Piano • Vocal • Guitar

CHRISTINA PERRI
HEAD OR HEART

ISBN 978-1-4803-9154-3

HAL•LEONARD®
CORPORATION
7777 W. BLUEMOUND RD. P.O. BOX 13819 MILWAUKEE, WI 53213

For all works contained herein:
Unauthorized copying, arranging, adapting, recording, Internet posting, public performance,
or other distribution of the printed music in this publication is an infringement of copyright.
Infringers are liable under the law.

Visit Hal Leonard Online at
www.halleonard.com

TRUST

Words and Music by
CHRISTINA PERRI

With motion

Copyright © 2014 Miss Perri Lane Publishing
All Rights Administered by Songs Of Kobalt Music Publishing
All Rights Reserved Used by Permission

___ that hurt the ones you're lov - ing,   ha - tred for who you're be - com -
- o - ries that won't stop sting - ing,   prom - is - es I could - n't be -

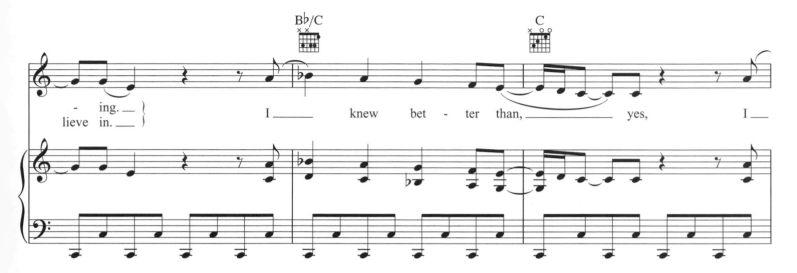

- ing. ___ }   I ___ knew bet - ter than, ___ yes,   I ___
lieve in. ___ }

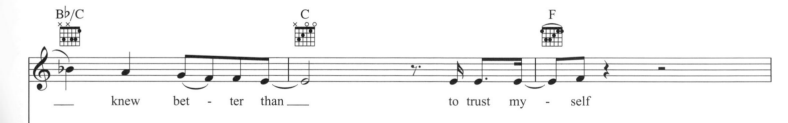

___ knew bet - ter than ___   to trust my - self

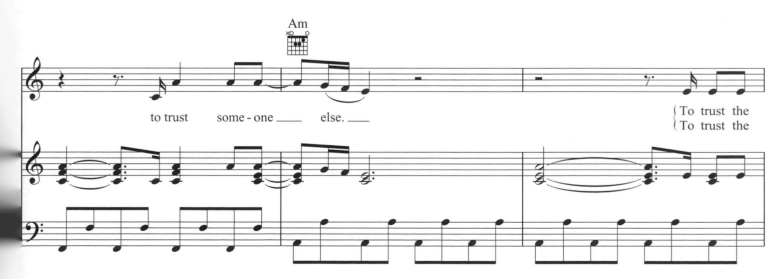

to trust   some - one ___ else. ___   { To trust the
{ To trust the

lies that slip from __ my mouth, trust the heart I'm so __ quick to sell.
doubt in the back of __ my mind, trust the trail of pain __ left be - hind. __

Yes, I knew bet - ter than, __

I knew __ bet - ter than to trust love a - gain. __

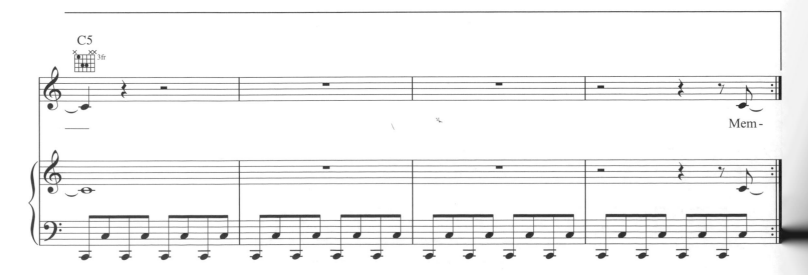

Mem -

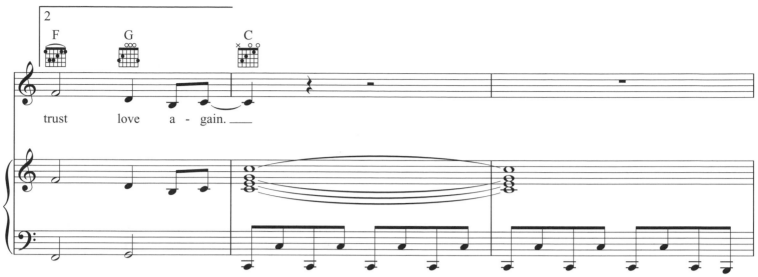

trust   love   a - gain. ____

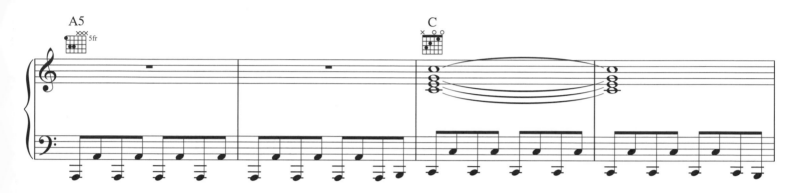

And   I'm   so   quick   to   lose _

____   what   was   nev - er   mine _   to   keep. ____   And

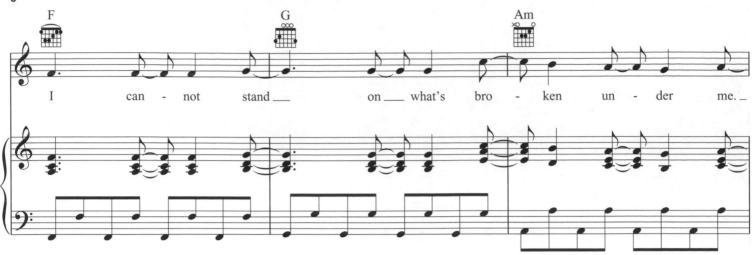

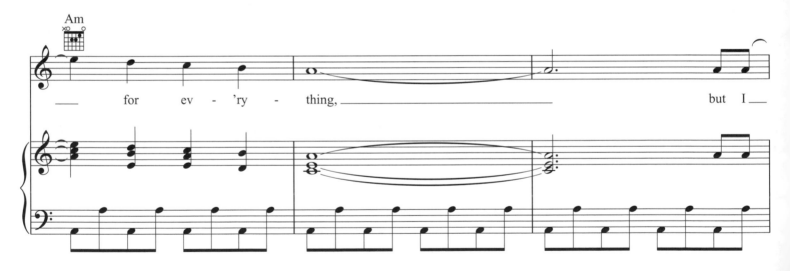

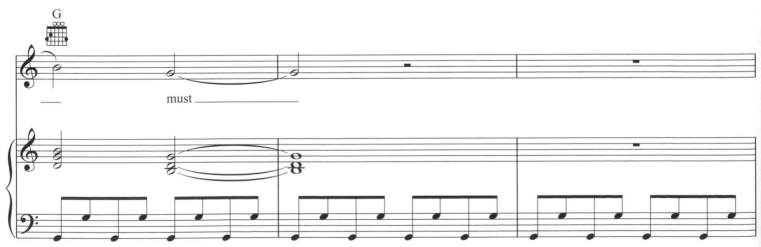

BURNING GOLD

Words and Music by CHRISTINA PERRI
and KID HARPOON

Moderate Pop

Copyright © 2014 Miss Perri Lane Publishing and Universal Music Publishing Ltd.
All Rights for Miss Perri Lane Publishing Administered by Songs Of Kobalt Music Publishing
All Rights for Universal Music Publishing Ltd. in the U.S. and Canada Controlled and Administered by Universal - PolyGram International Publishing, Inc.
All Rights Reserved   Used by Permission

I can see my fu-ture slip a-way. ____ Hon-ey, you won't get there if you
I can see my chance be-gin to fade. ____ One ____ step for-ward and two

don't be-lieve. ____ } I wish the wind would car-ry a change. __ I've had e-nough. __
back a-gain, ____ }

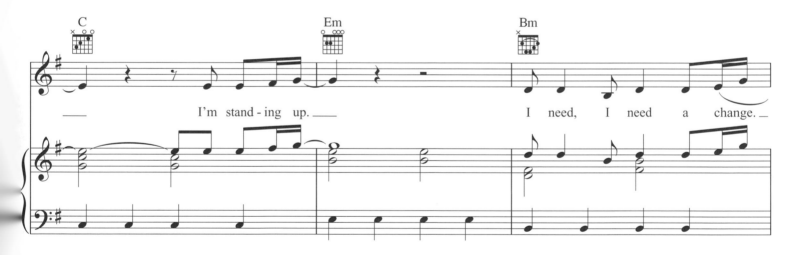

____ I'm stand-ing up. ____ I need, I need a change. __

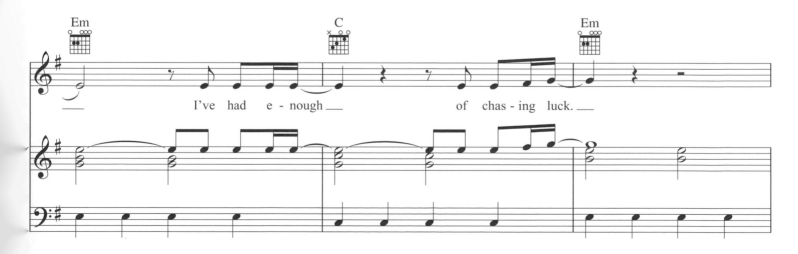

____ I've had e-nough ____ of chas-ing luck. __

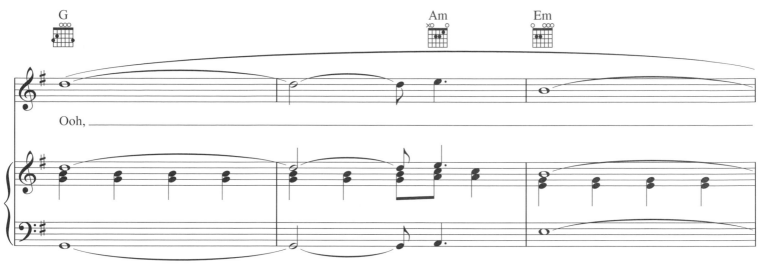

Ooh,

look-ing back I see I had the flame in me.

I'm the wind that's car-ry-ing change. I've had e-nough of chas-ing luck.

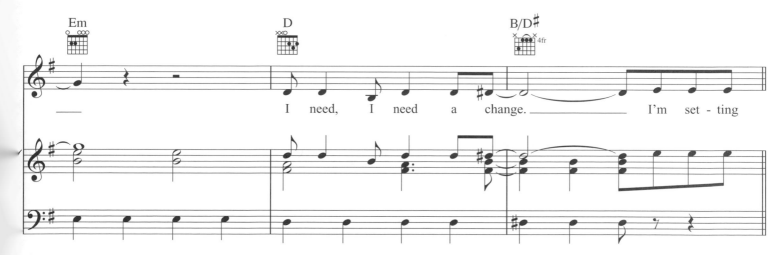

I need, I need a change. I'm set-ting

fire to the life that I know. _____ We start a fire ev -'ry-where that we go. _

_____ We're start-ing fires, _____ we're start-ing fires _ 'til our

lives are burn - ing gold. _____ I'm set - ting   lives are burn - ing gold. ____

_ 'Til our lives are burn - ing gold. _____

BE MY FOREVER

Words and Music by CHRISTINA PERRI
and JAMIE SCOTT

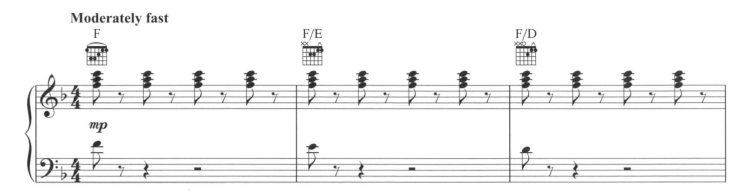

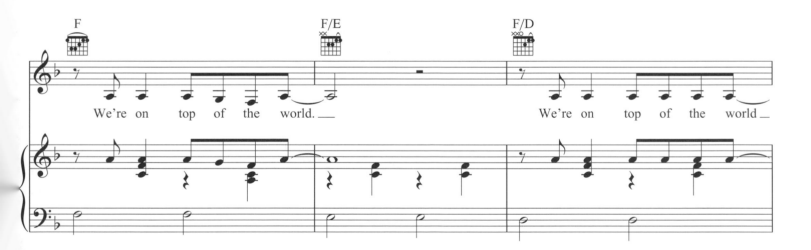

We're on top of the world. __ We're on top of the world __

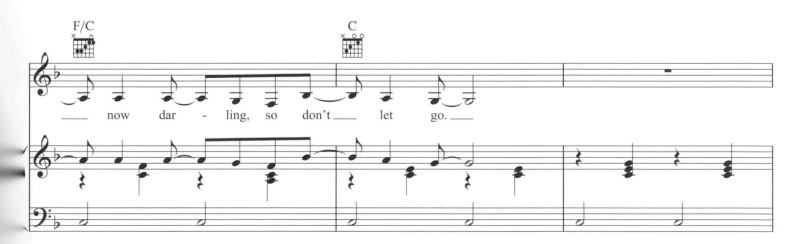

__ now dar-ling, so don't __ let go. __

Copyright © 2013 Miss Perri Lane Publishing and EMI Music Publishing UK Ltd.
All Rights for Miss Perri Lane Publishing Administered by Songs Of Kobalt Music Publishing
All Rights for EMI Music Publishing UK Ltd. Administered by Sony/ATV Music Publishing LLC, 8 Music Square West, Nashville, TN 37203
All Rights Reserved   Used by Permission

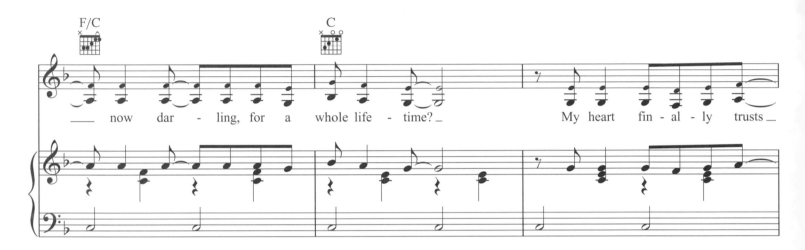

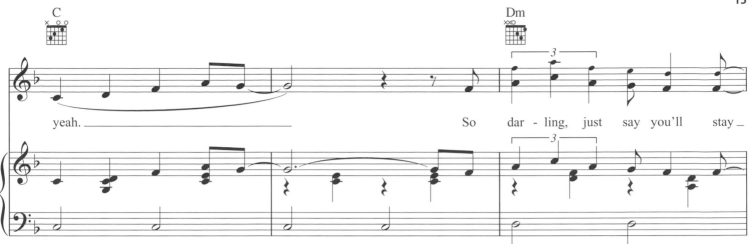

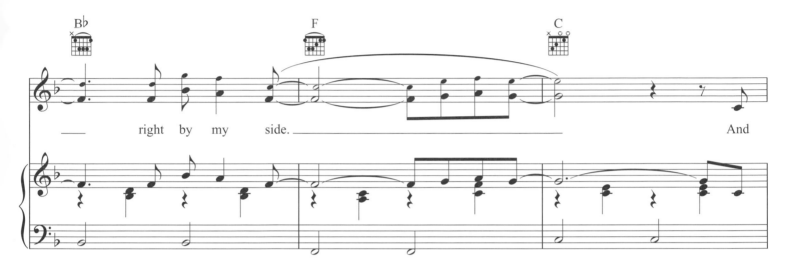

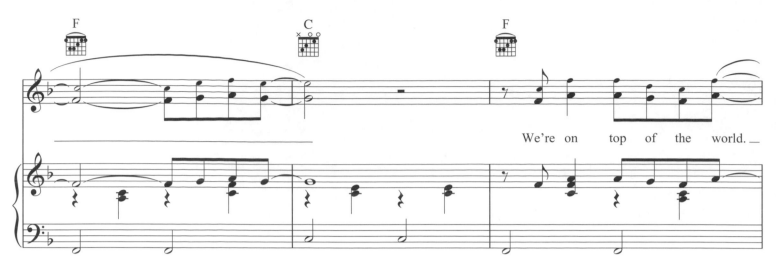

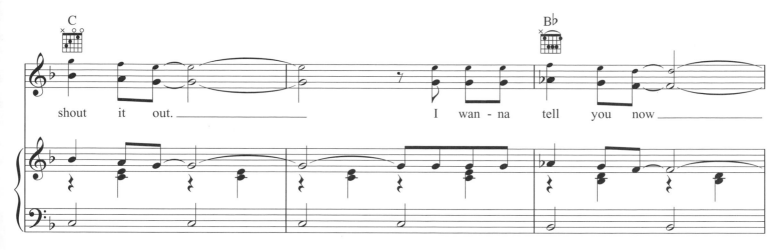

shout it out. _____ I wan - na tell you now _____

_____ 'cause I know ____ some - how ____ it's right. _____ And

oh, _____ we got time, yeah. _____

_____ So dar - ling, just say you'll stay ____ right by my side. ___

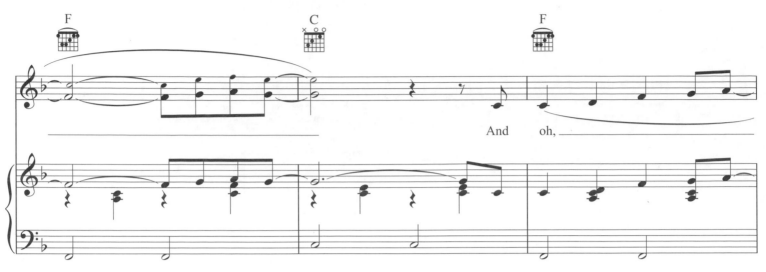

And oh,

we got love, yeah. So

dar - ling, just swear you'll stand right by my side.

Be my for - ev - er. Be my for - ev - er. Be my for -

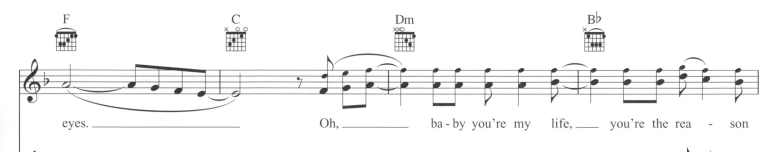

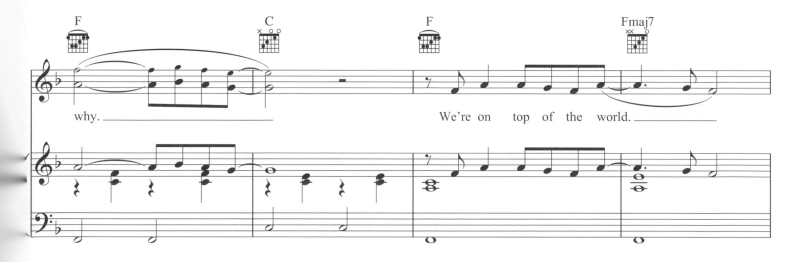

We're on top of the world ___ now dar - ling, so don't ___ let go. ___

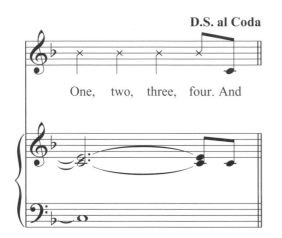

D.S. al Coda

One, two, three, four. And

CODA

ev - er. ___ Will you love me for -

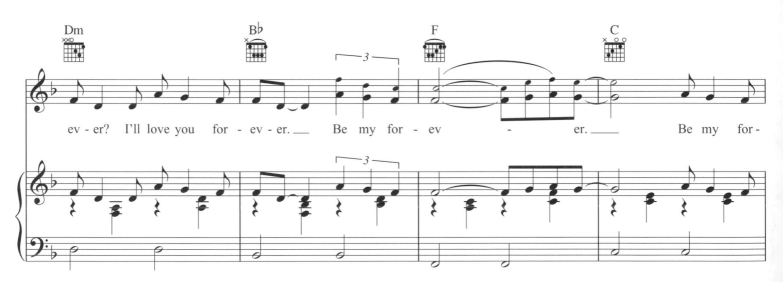

ev - er? I'll love you for - ev - er. ___ Be my for - ev - er. ___ Be my for -

ev - er. Be my for - ev - er. Be my for - ev - er. ___

HUMAN

Words and Music by CHRISTINA PERRI
and MARTIN JOHNSON

Copyright © 2013 Miss Perri Lane Publishing, EMI April Music Inc. and Martin Music Inc.
All Rights for Miss Perri Lane Publishing Administered by Songs Of Kobalt Music Publishing
All Rights for EMI April Music Inc. and Martin Music Inc. Administered by Sony/ATV Music Publishing LLC, 8 Music Square West, Nashville, TN 37203
All Rights Reserved   Used by Permission

be ___ your num - ber one. ___
give ___ you all ___ I ___ am. ___ I can

do it, ___ I can do it, ___ I can

do it. _____ But I'm on - ly

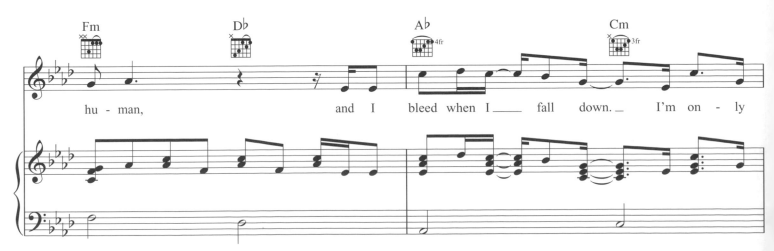

hu - man, ___ and I bleed when I ___ fall down. ___ I'm on - ly

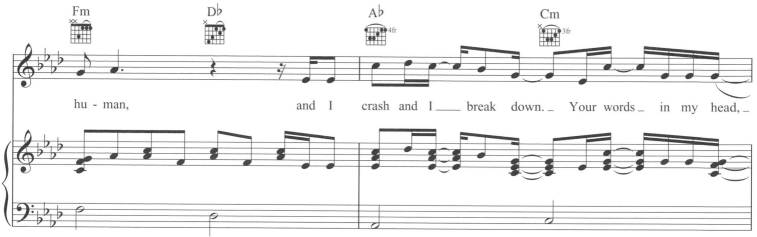

hu - man, and I crash and I ___ break down. Your words ___ in my head, ___

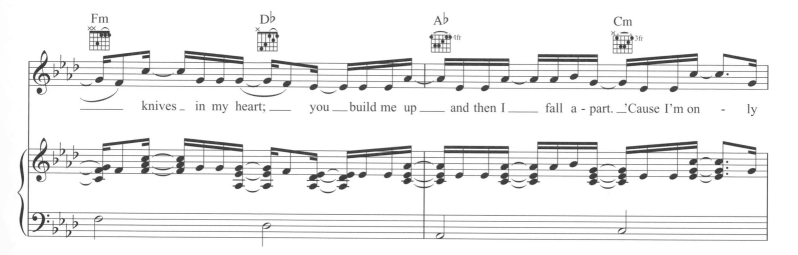

___ knives ___ in my heart; ___ you ___ build me up ___ and then I ___ fall a - part. 'Cause I'm on — ly

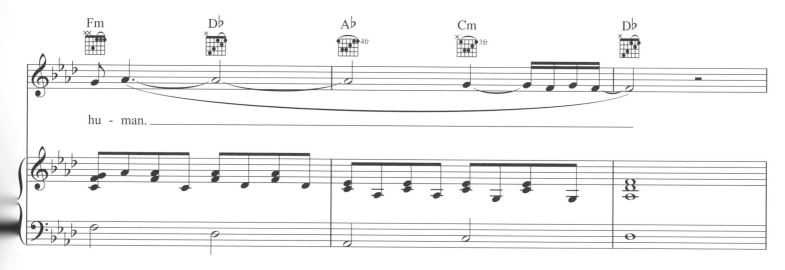

hu - man. _____

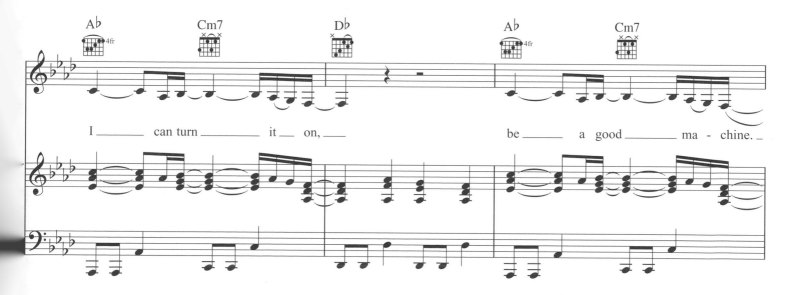

I _____ can turn _____ it ___ on, ___ be _____ a good _____ ma - chine. ___

I can hold__ the weight__ of worlds__ if

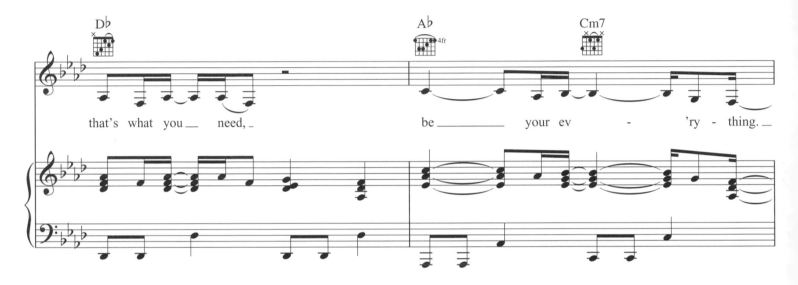

that's what you__ need,__ be_____ your ev - 'ry - thing.__

I can do it, I can

do it, I'll get through it._____ But I'm on - ly

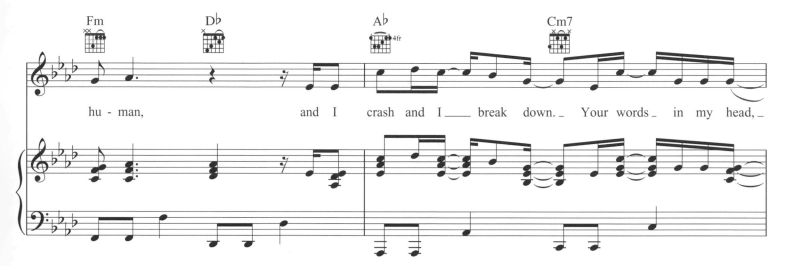

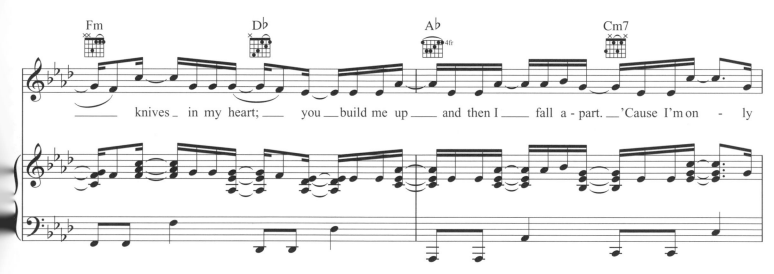

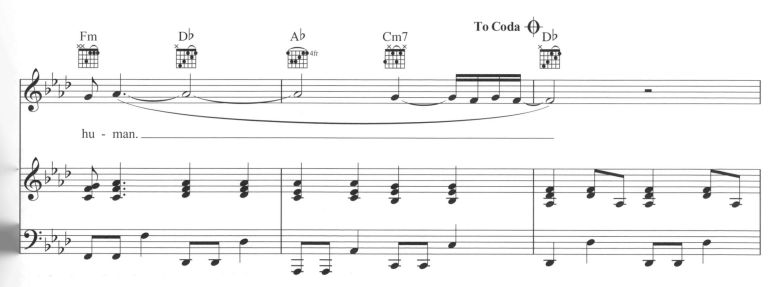

I'm on - ly hu - man, I'm on - ly hu - man, just a lit - tle

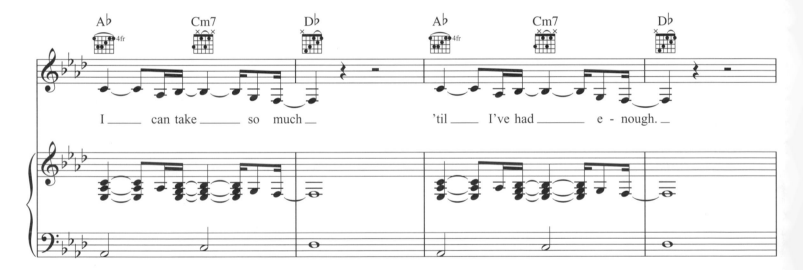

hu - man. _____

I ___ can take ___ so much ___ 'til ___ I've had ___ e - nough. __

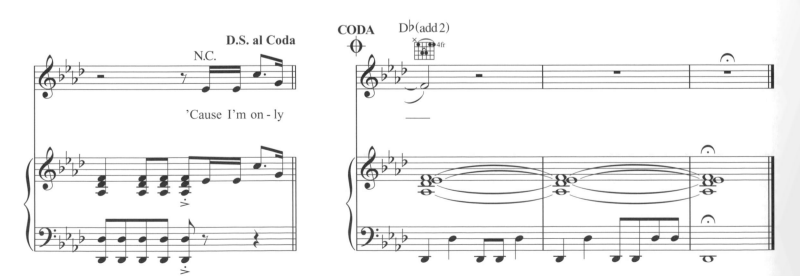

D.S. al Coda

N.C.

'Cause I'm on - ly

CODA D♭(add 2)

ONE NIGHT

Words and Music by CHRISTINA PERRI
and KEVIN GRIFFIN

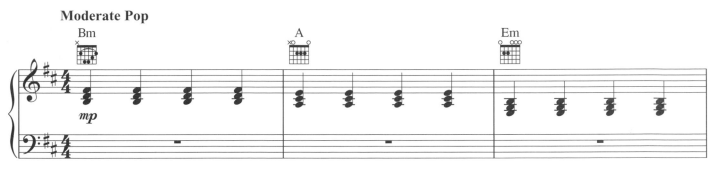

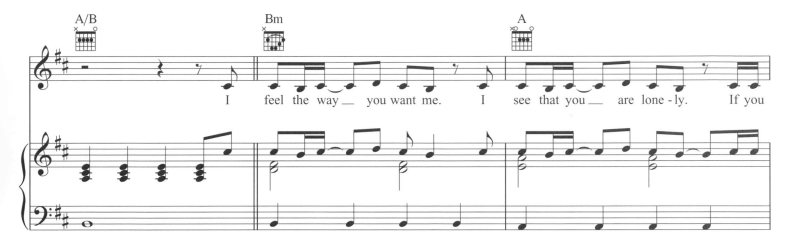

I feel the way __ you want me. I see that you __ are lone-ly. If you

could, I know __ you'd leave with me. __ It's more than cur-i-o-si-ty. __ And I've

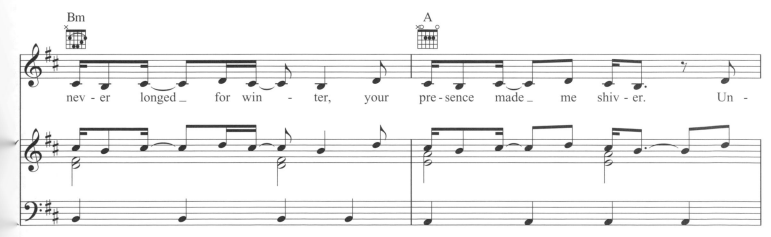

nev-er longed __ for win-ter, your pre-sence made __ me shiv-er. Un-

Copyright © 2014 Miss Perri Lane Publishing and Control Group Music
All Rights for Miss Perri Lane Publishing Administered by Songs Of Kobalt Music Publishing
All Rights for Control Group Music Administered by BMG Rights Management (US) LLC
All Rights Reserved   Used by Permission

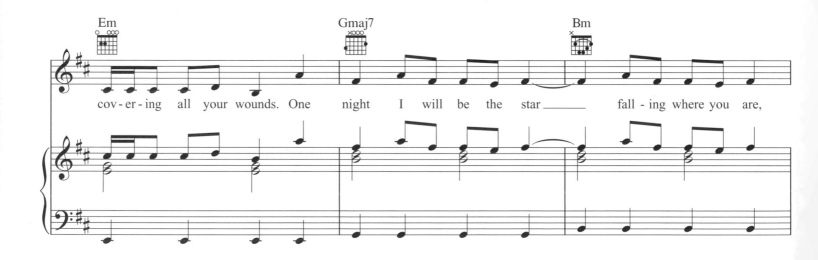

night. One night, one night, one night. You've

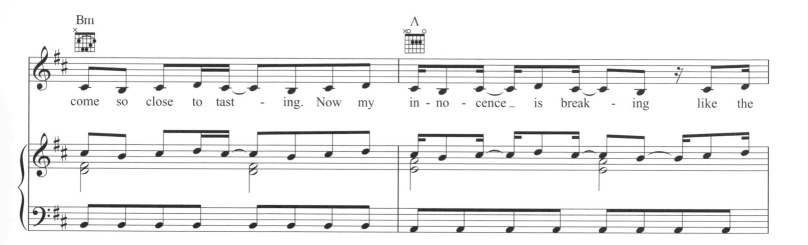

come so close to tast - ing. Now my in - no - cence_ is break - ing like the

o - cean in a per - fect storm,_ it makes me want you e - ven more._ And I've

nev - er been_ so jeal - ous. I've nev - er felt_ so help - less, so

night, one night, one night. _____ Hur - ry, the sun _____

_____ is wak - ing. _____ Dar - ling, don't leave _____ me wait - ing. _____

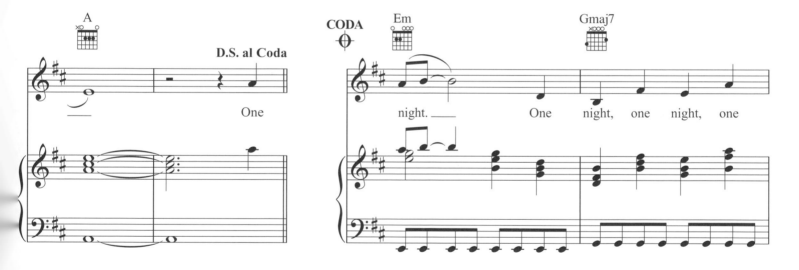

_____ One

night. _____ One night, one night, one

night. One night, one night, one night. _____

I DON'T WANNA BREAK

Words and Music by CHRISTINA PERRI
and JACK ANTONOFF

Copyright © 2013 Miss Perri Lane Publishing, Sony/ATV Music Publishing LLC and Ducky Donath Music
All Rights for Miss Perri Lane Publishing Administered by Songs Of Kobalt Music Publishing
All Rights for Sony/ATV Music Publishing LLC and Ducky Donath Music Administered by Sony/ATV Music Publishing LLC, 8 Music Square West, Nashville, TN 37203
All Rights Reserved   Used by Permission

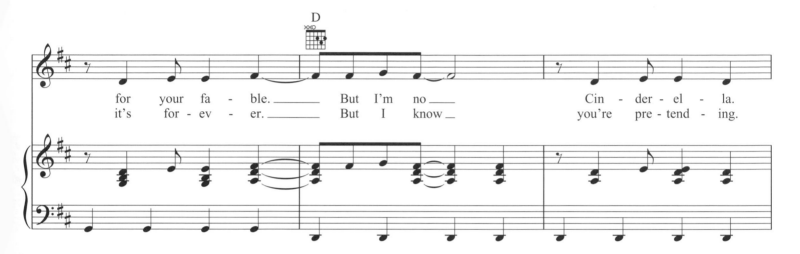

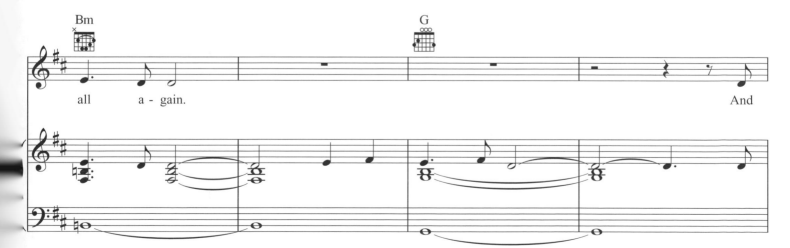

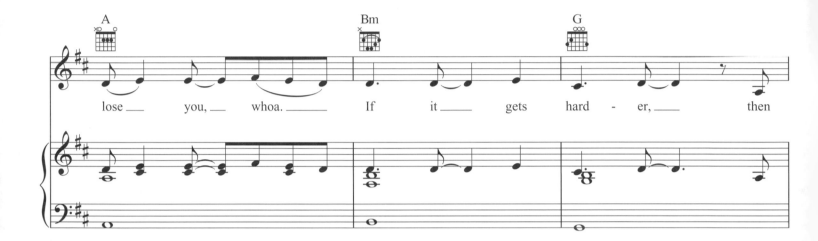

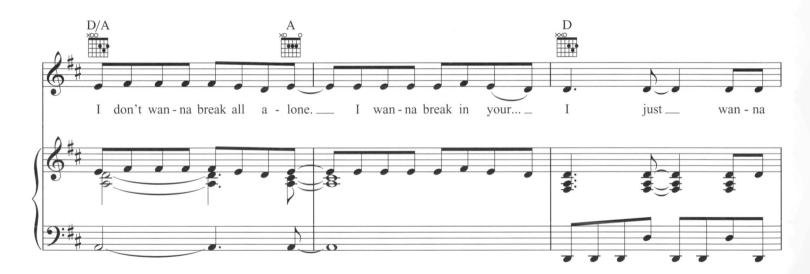

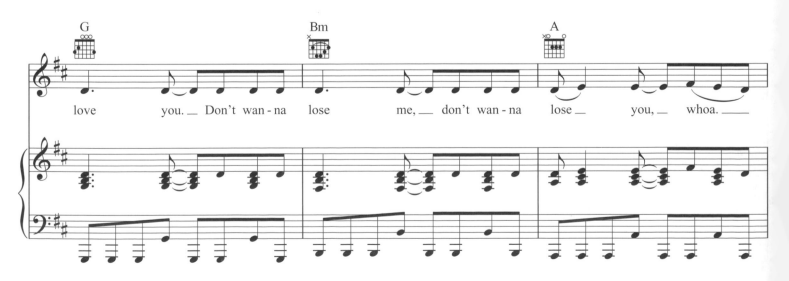

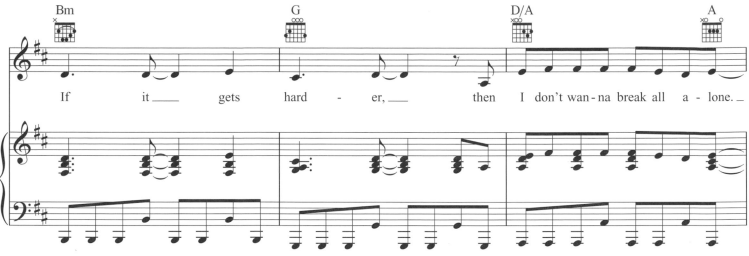

If it ___ gets hard - er, ___ then I don't wan-na break all a - lone. ___

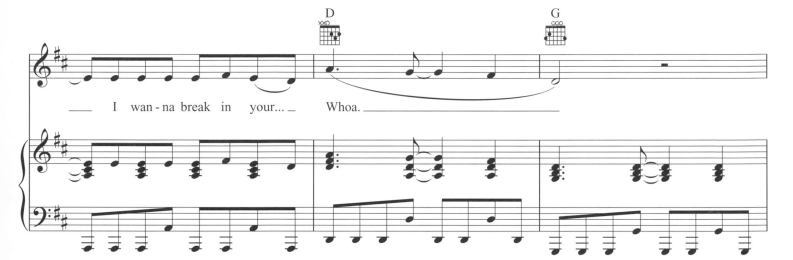

___ I wan - na break in your... ___ Whoa. ___

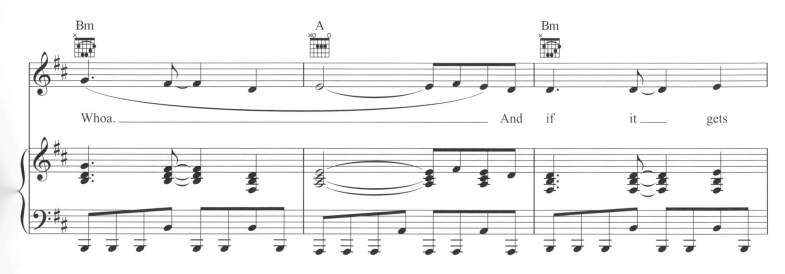

Whoa. ___ And if it ___ gets

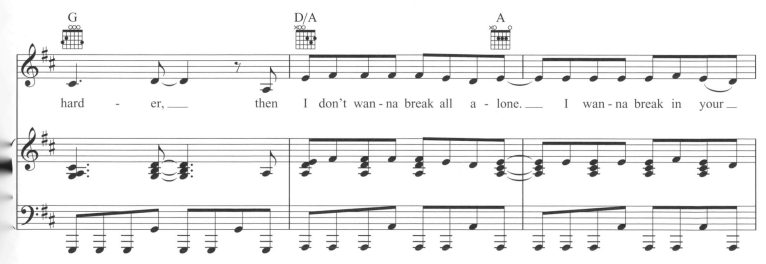

hard - er, ___ then I don't wan-na break all a - lone. ___ I wan-na break in your ___

I wan-na break in your... Whoa.

Whoa. And if it gets

hard - er, then I don't wan-na break all a - lone. I wan-na break in your...

Whoa, whoa.

whoa. _____
arms. _____ Don't wan - na break in your... _

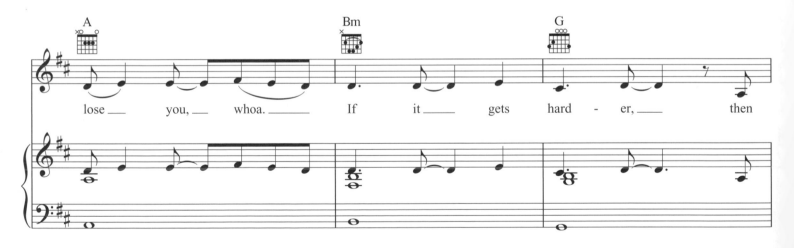

I just __ wan - na love you. __ Don't wan - na lose me, __ don't wan - na

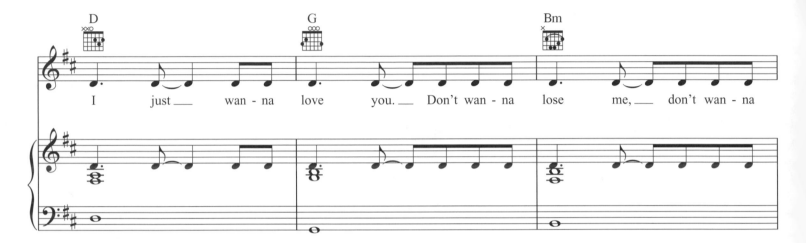

lose __ you, __ whoa. _____ If it __ gets hard - er, ____ then

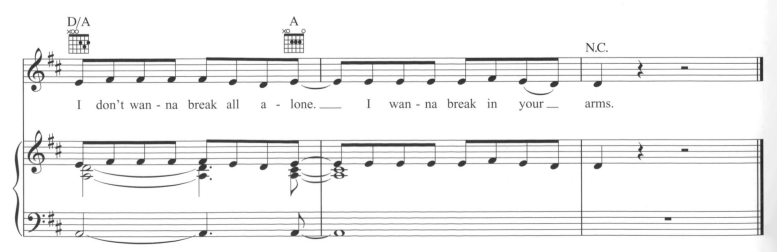

I don't wan - na break all a - lone. __ I wan - na break in your __ arms.

SEA OF LOVERS

Words and Music by CHRISTINA PERRI
and JAMES ELIOT

Moderate Pop Rock

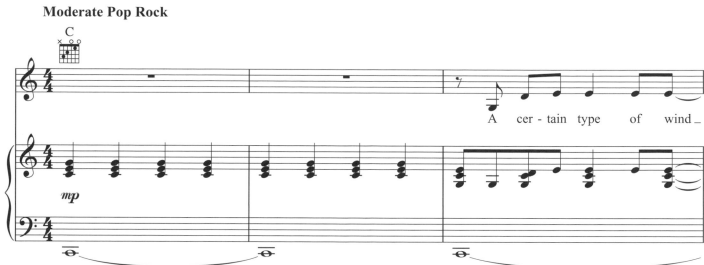

A cer-tain type of wind _

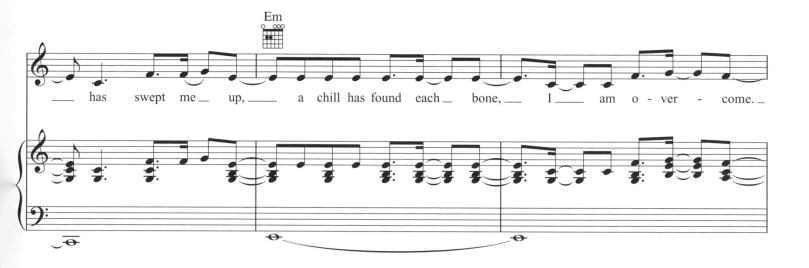

_ has swept me _ up, _ a chill has found each _ bone, _ I _ am o-ver-come. _

_ There is an i-cy breath _ that _ es-capes my _ lips _ and I am lost a-gain. _

Copyright © 2014 Miss Perri Lane Publishing and Sony/ATV Tunes LLC
All Rights for Miss Perri Lane Publishing Administered by Songs Of Kobalt Music Publishing
All Rights for Sony/ATV Tunes LLC Administered by Sony/ATV Music Publishing LLC, 8 Music Square West, Nashville, TN 37203
All Rights Reserved   Used by Permission

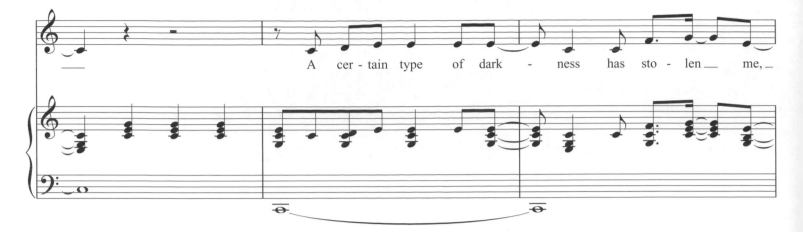

A cer - tain type of dark - ness has sto - len __ me, __

__ un - der a qui - et mask __ of un - cer - tain - ty. __ I wait for light like wa -

- ter from the sky __ and I am lost a - gain. __ In the sea __

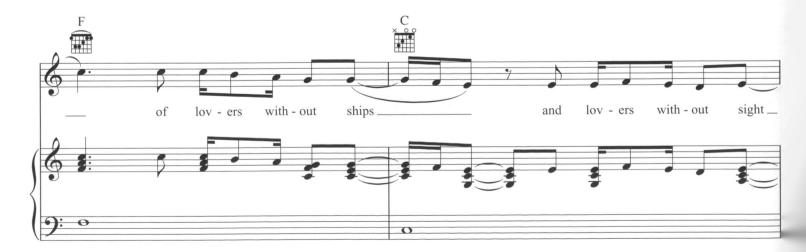

__ of lov - ers with - out ships _____ and lov - ers with - out sight __

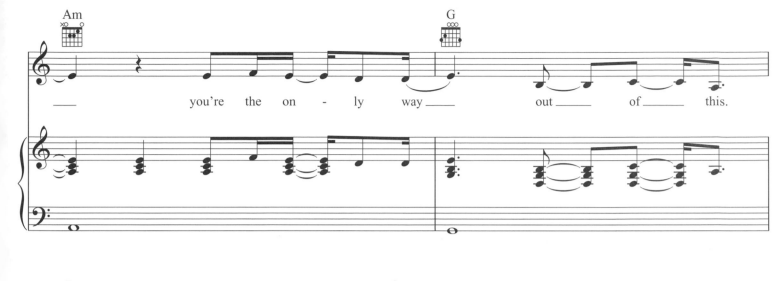

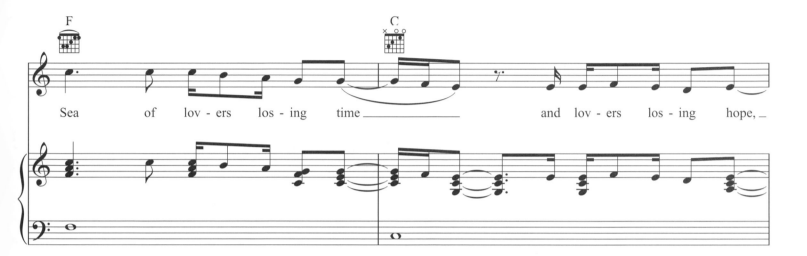

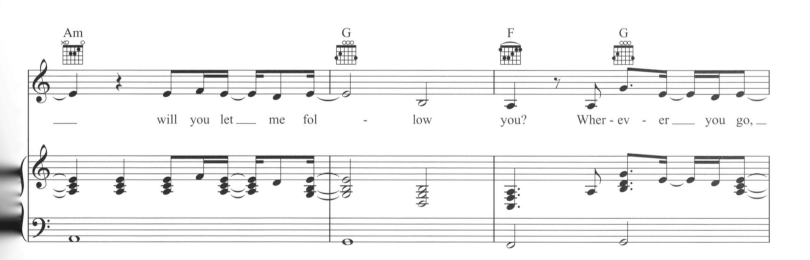

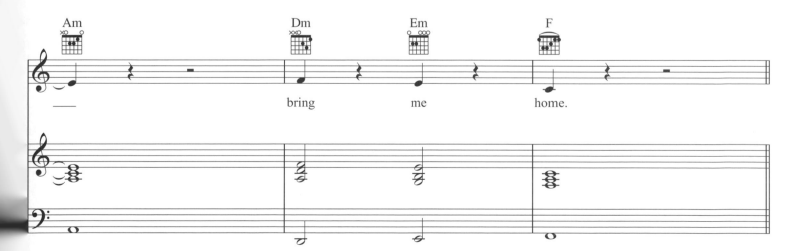

A cer - tain type of si - lence has filled my __ voice, __
A cer - tain type of wind __ has swept me __ up, __

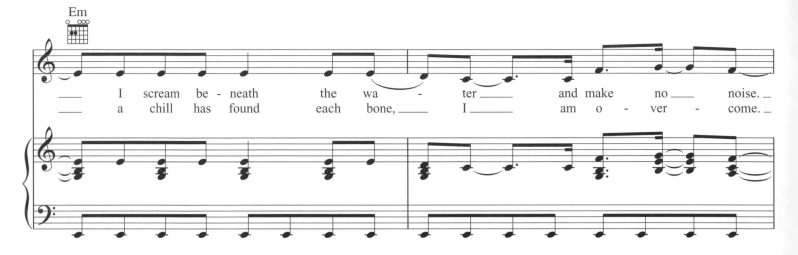

__ I scream be - neath the wa - ter __ and make no __ noise. _
__ a chill has found each bone, __ I __ am o - ver - come. _

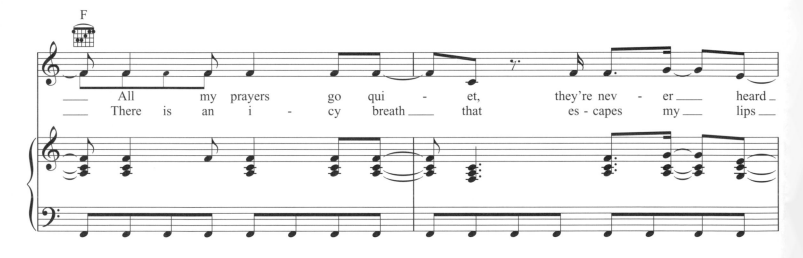

__ All my prayers go qui - et, they're nev - er __ heard __
There is an i - cy breath __ that es - capes my __ lips __

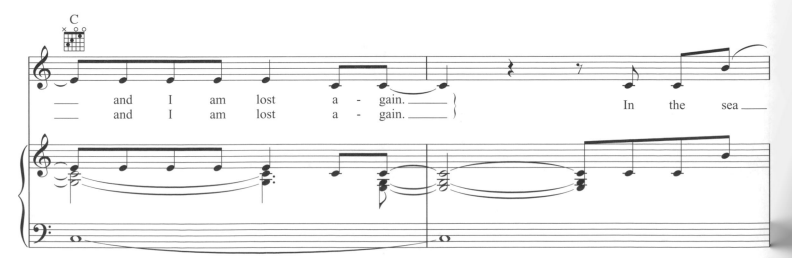

__ and I am lost a - gain. __
__ and I am lost a - gain. __
In the sea __

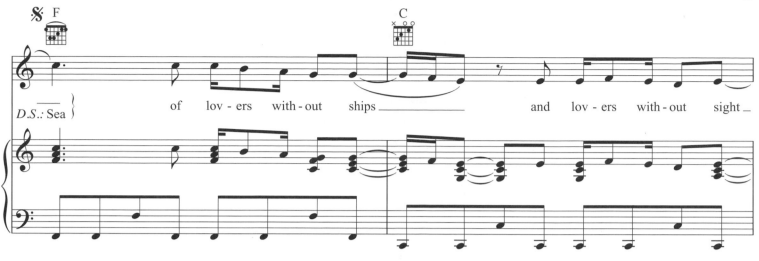

of lov-ers with-out ships _____ and lov-ers with-out sight _____

D.S.: Sea

_____ you're the on-ly way _____ out _____ of _____ this.

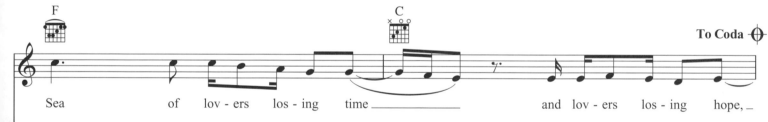

To Coda ⊕

Sea of lov-ers los-ing time _____ and lov-ers los-ing hope, _____

1

_____ will you let _____ me fol - low

THE WORDS

Words and Music by CHRISTINA PERRI,
DAVID HODGES and DAVID RYAN HARRIS

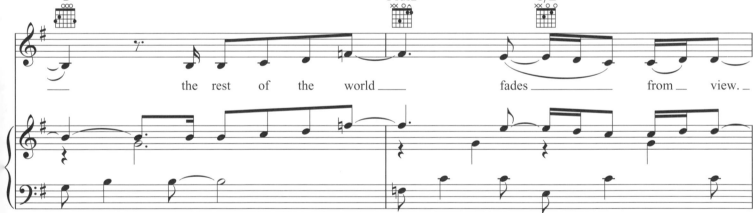

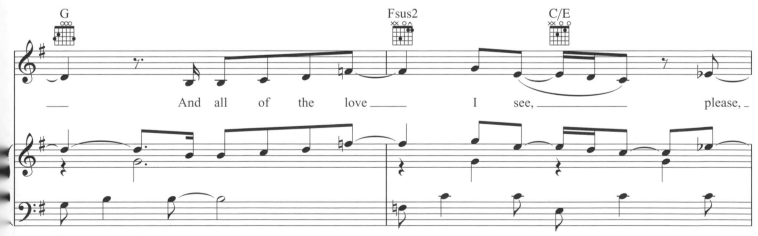

Recorded a half-step lower

Copyright © 2014 Miss Perri Lane Publishing, 3 Weddings Music and Peace Pourage Music
All Rights for Miss Perri Lane Publishing and 3 Weddings Music Administered by Songs Of Kobalt Music Publishing
All Rights Reserved   Used by Permission

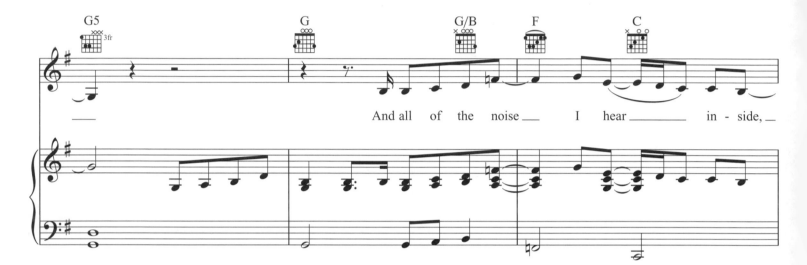

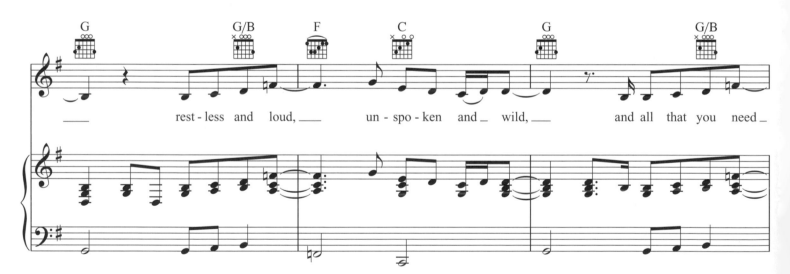

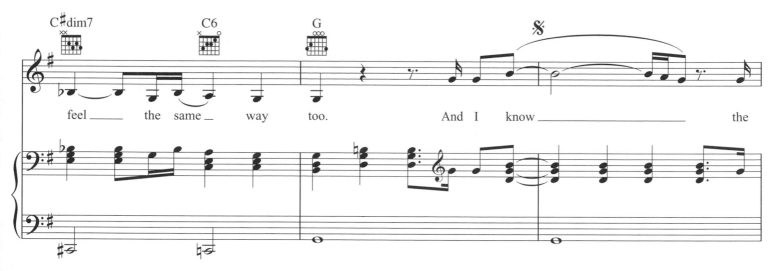

feel ___ the same ___ way too. And I know _____ the

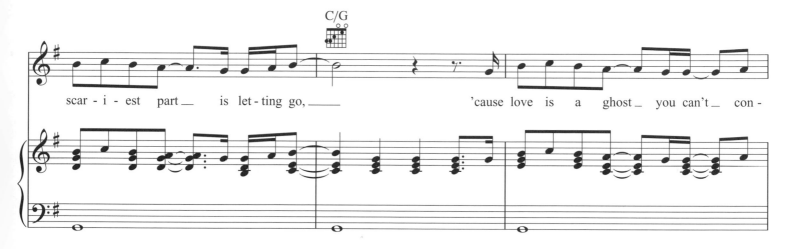

scar - i - est part ___ is let - ting go, ___ 'cause love is a ghost ___ you can't ___ con -

trol. _____ I prom - ise you the truth ___ can't hurt us now, so let the

words slip out ___ of your mouth. ___

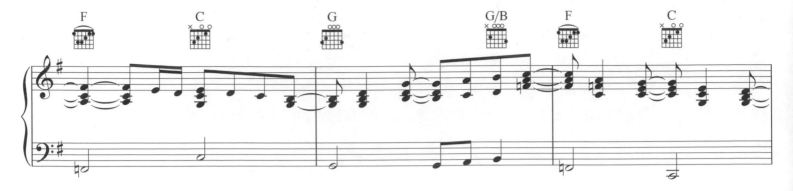

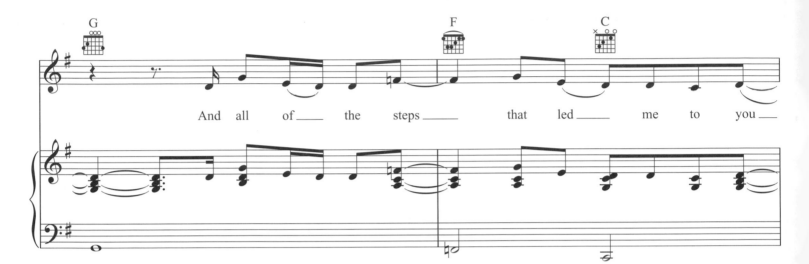

And all of ___ the steps ___ that led ___ me to you ___

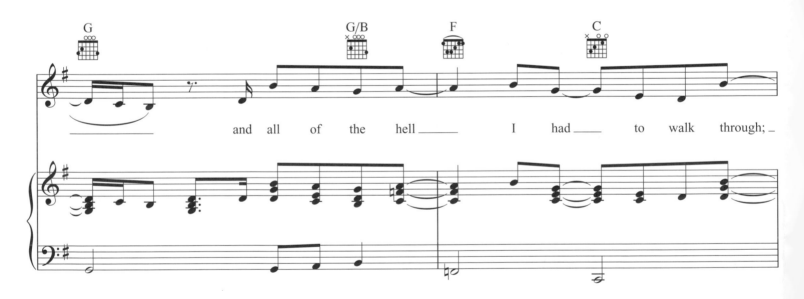

___ and all of the hell ___ I had ___ to walk through; _

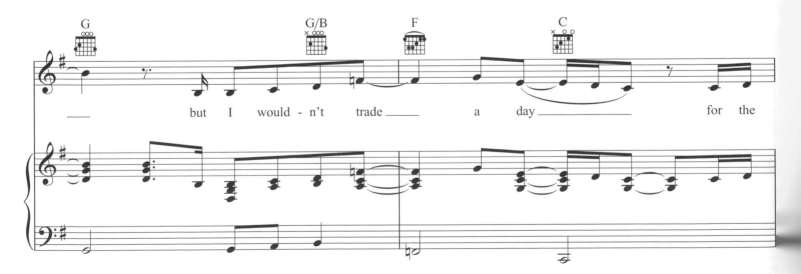

___ but I would-n't trade ___ a day ___ for the

chance __ to say _____ my love, ___ I'm in love __ with you. ___ And I know __

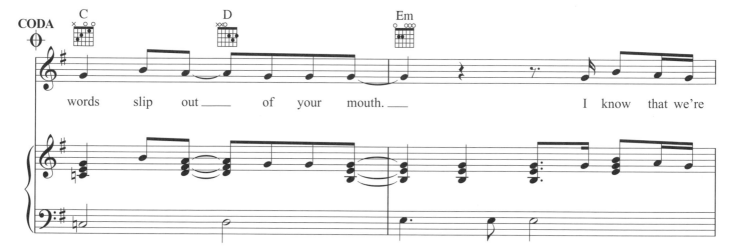

words slip out _____ of your mouth. ___ I know that we're

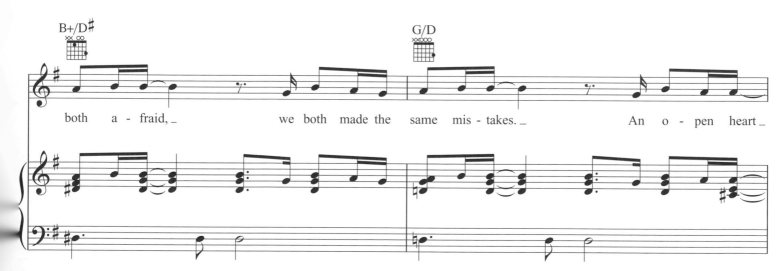

both a-fraid, _ we both made the same mis-takes. _ An o-pen heart _

_____ is an o-pen wound _ to you. _____ And in the wind of a

heav-y choice, ___ love ___ has a qui-et voice. ___ Still your mind, ___

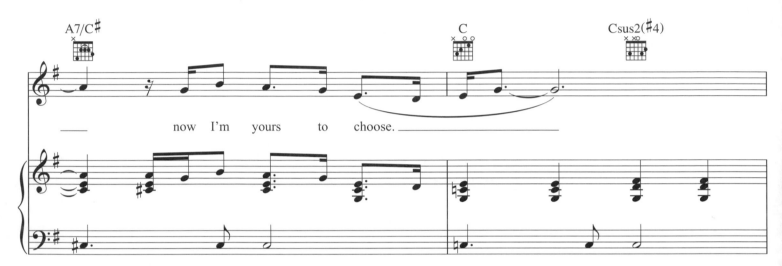

___ now I'm yours to choose. _____

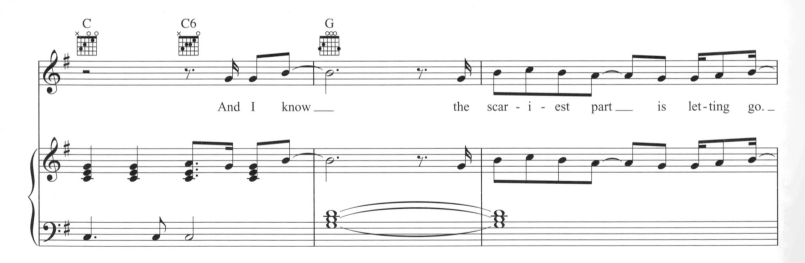

And I know ___ the scar-i-est part ___ is let-ting go. ___

___ Let my love be the light ___ that guides ___ you home. And I ___

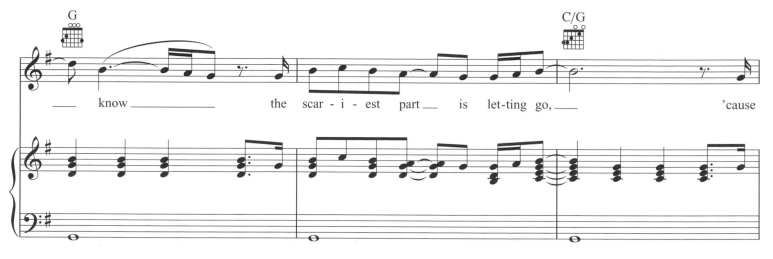

know _____ the scar - i - est part ___ is let-ting go, ____ 'cause

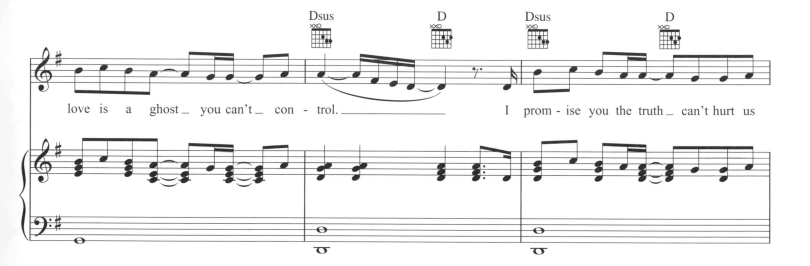

love is a ghost ___ you can't ___ con - trol. _____ I prom - ise you the truth ___ can't hurt us

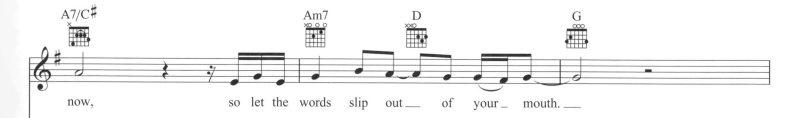

now, _____ so let the words slip out ___ of your ___ mouth. ___

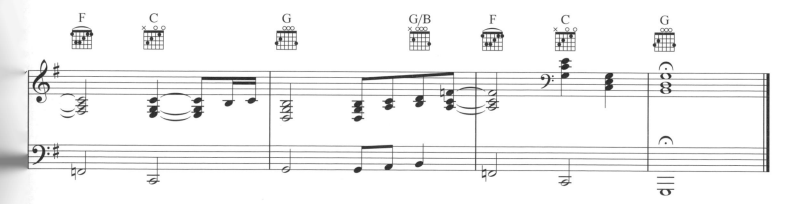

LONELY CHILD

Words and Music by CHRISTINA PERRI
and KEVIN GRIFFIN

Moderate Latin groove

Just as fast as you

came, just as fast as the sun - set, you

pushed me a - way. You pushed me down, down, down, down,

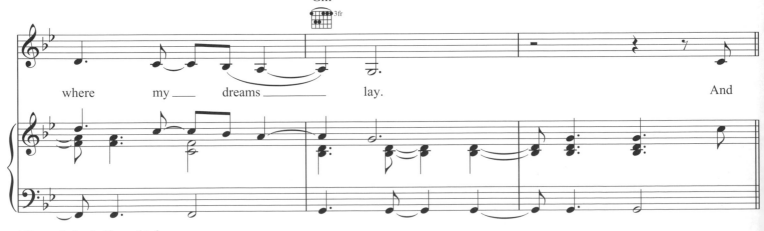

where my dreams lay. And

Recorded a half step higher.

Copyright © 2014 Miss Perri Lane Publishing and Control Group Music
All Rights for Miss Perri Lane Publishing Administered by Songs Of Kobalt Music Publishing
All Rights for Control Group Music Administered by BMG Rights Management (US) LLC
All Rights Reserved   Used by Permission

just as quick as you ____ left, ____ just as quick as you
Just as dark as the ____ night, ____ just as dark as the

left, my heart ____ un dressed, ____ and I fell down, _
night when __ I __ lost my mind, I lost con - trol.

down, __ down, down. You took my wish __ back to the well.
Down, __ down, down, you let me sell my love for my soul.

And I re - mem - ber all the words that you __
And I re - mem - ber all the words that you __

said. _____
wrote. _____
That love is just a
That love is just a

spark that starts in your heart and ends in your head.
sound that plays in your heart and gets caught in your throat.

Dar - ling, come _____ down, come _____ down, you'll

lose your-self in the clouds. Slow _____ down,

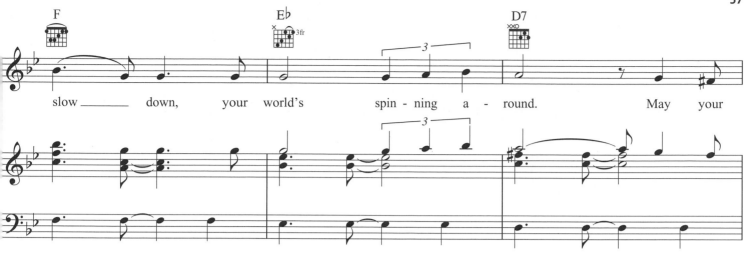

slow _____ down, your world's spin - ning a - round. May your

un - tamed heart stay rest - less, ___ run - ning

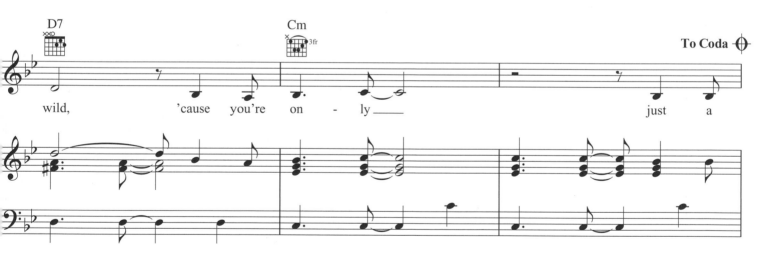

To Coda

wild, 'cause you're on - ly ___ just a

lone - ly, lone - ly child.

And I re-mem-ber

Instrumental ends

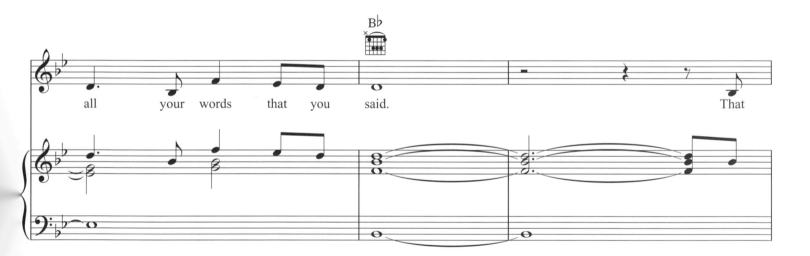

all your words that you said. That

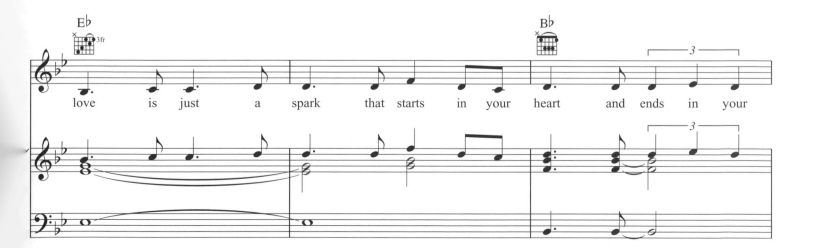

love is just a spark that starts in your heart and ends in your

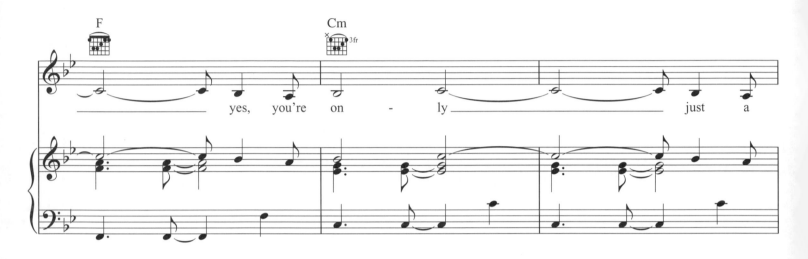

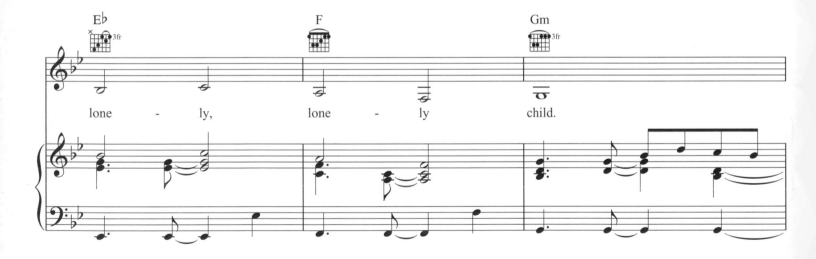

RUN

Words and Music by
CHRISTINA PERRI

Copyright © 2014 Miss Perri Lane Publishing
All Rights Administered by Songs Of Kobalt Music Publishing
All Rights Reserved   Used by Permission

ev - 'ry - bod - y ____ else. ____

Please move that ___ fin - ger ____ that's been point - ing to my mis - takes. _

I want no part in the feel - ings your ___ words ___ make. ____ So let ___

____ go, ____ yeah, ____ let me love ____ you ___ to - day. ___

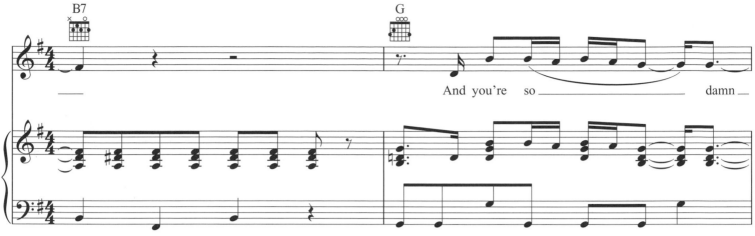

And you're so _____ damn ____

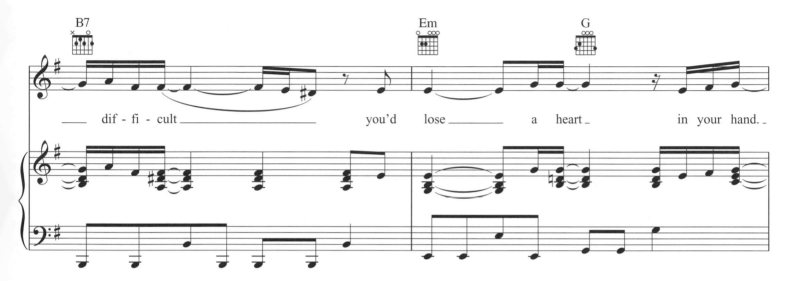

____ dif - fi - cult _____ you'd lose _____ a heart ____ in your hand. ____

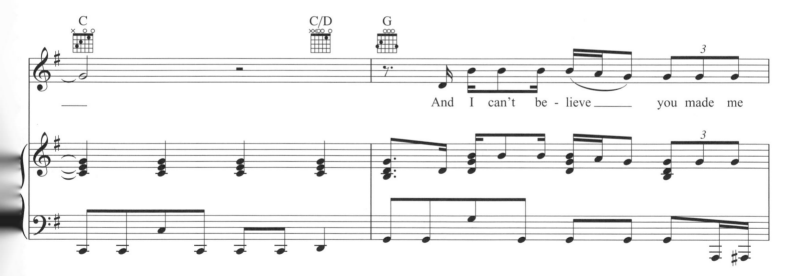

____ And I can't be - lieve _____ you made me

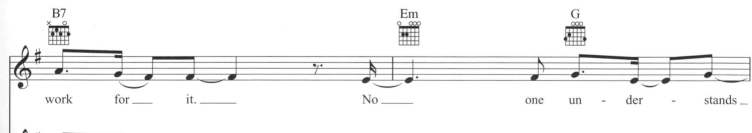

work for ___ it. ____ No _____ one un - der - stands ____

why I ___ don't run ___ as fast as I ___

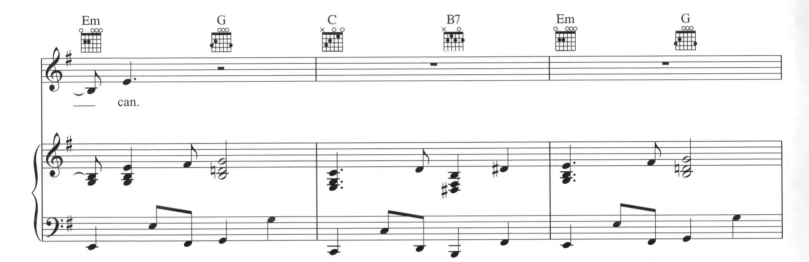

___ can.

And I can feel ___ ev - 'ry - thing, I can

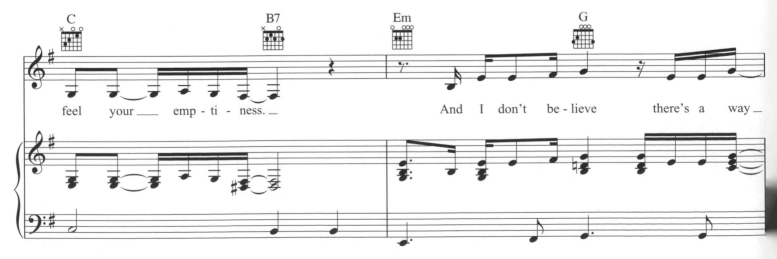

feel your ___ emp - ti - ness. ___ And I don't be - lieve there's a way ___

out of this ____ mess. ____ Un - less I ____ can for -

give ____ all your _ sins, ____ I ____ won't learn, _ I'll nev - er

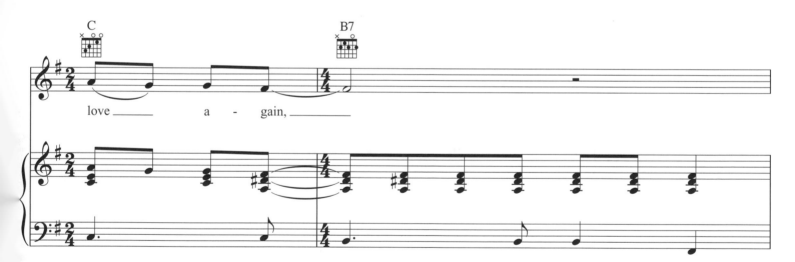

love ____ a - gain, ____

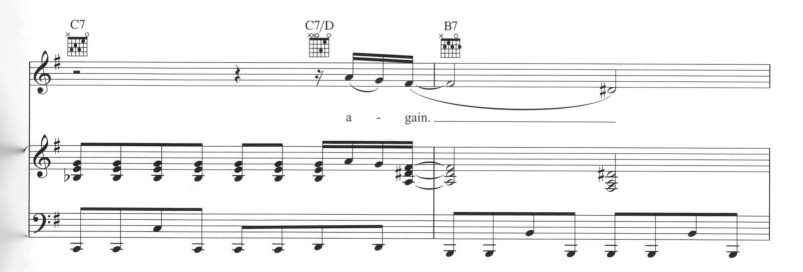

a - gain. _____

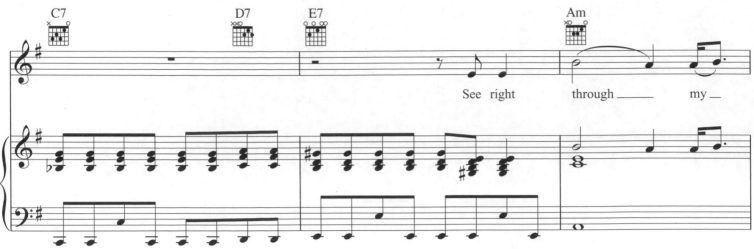

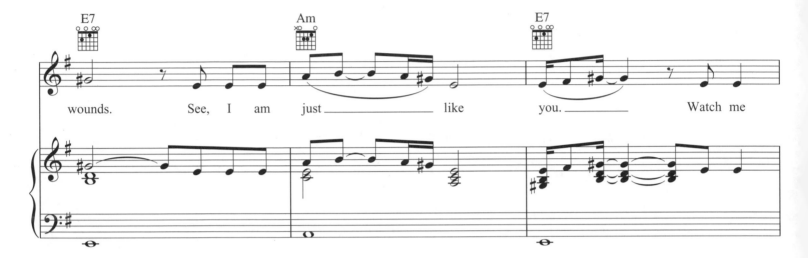

work for —— it. —— No —— one —— un - der - stands ——

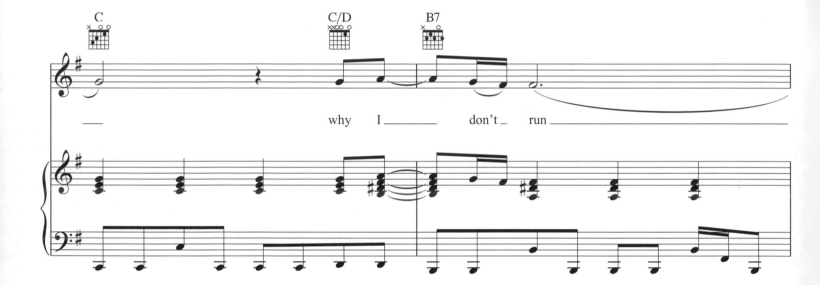

—— why I —————— don't —— run ——————————————

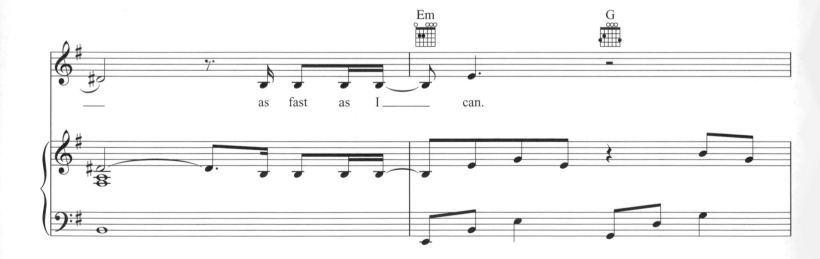

—— as fast as I —————— can.

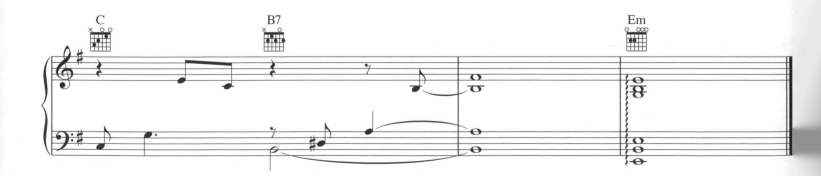

BUTTERFLY

Words and Music by
CHRISTINA PERRI

Slow Ballad

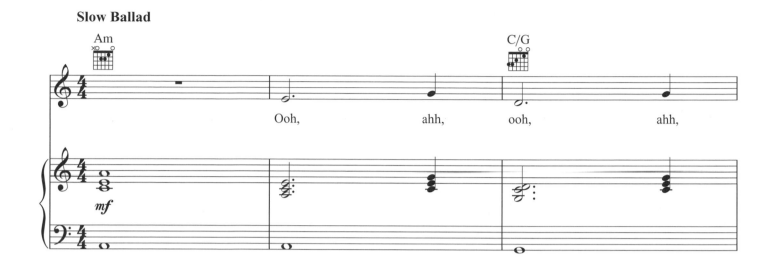

Ooh, ahh, ooh, ahh,

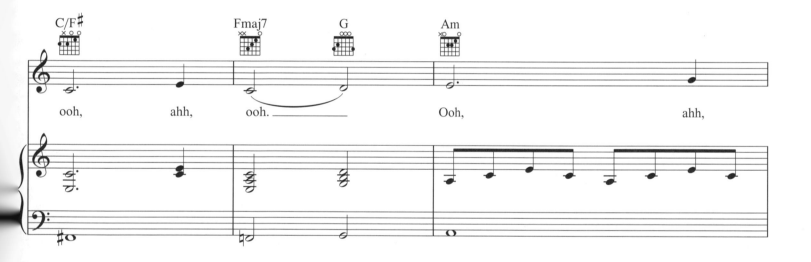

ooh, ahh, ooh. _____ Ooh, ahh,

ooh, ahh, ooh, ahh, ooh. _____

Copyright © 2014 Miss Perri Lane Publishing
All Rights Administered by Songs Of Kobalt Music Publishing
All Rights Reserved   Used by Permission

You're __ a pret - ty __ but - ter - fly, __ and you _____ keep on _____ pass - ing __ by. You'll
you're __ a pret - ty __ but - ter - fly, __ and I _____ be - lieved __ all your __ lies. I'm

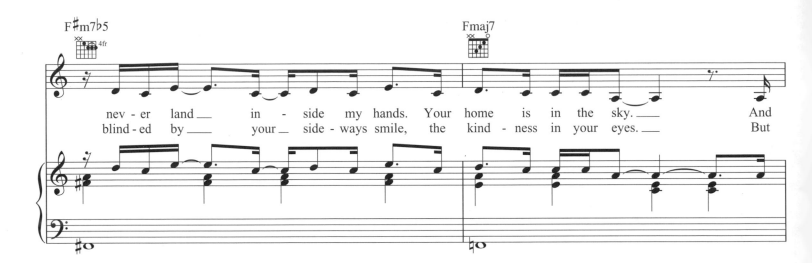

nev - er land __ in - side my hands. Your home is in the sky. __ And
blind - ed by __ your __ side - ways smile, the kind - ness in your eyes. __ But

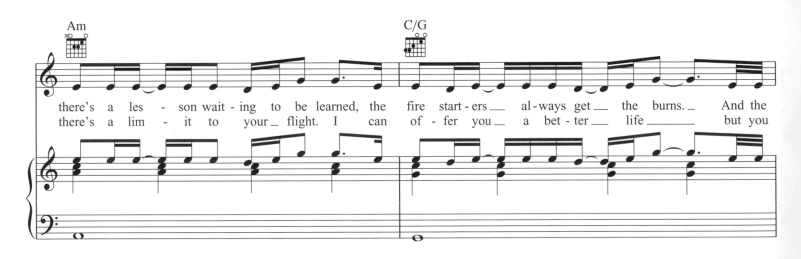

there's a les - son wait - ing to be learned, the fire start - ers __ al - ways get __ the burns. __ And the
there's a lim - it to your __ flight. I can of - fer you __ a bet - ter life _____ but you

good guys __ nev - er __ get the girl __ and shoot - ing stars __ can - not fix the world. __ } And
keep on __ fly - ing __ from the light, __ and I've lost my faith __ in __ wrong and right. __

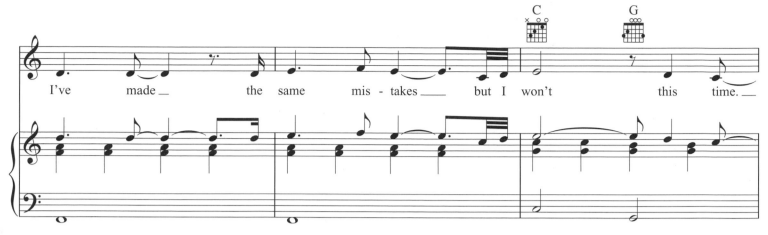

I've made __ the same mis - takes __ but I won't __ this time. __

__ No, I won't __ this time. __

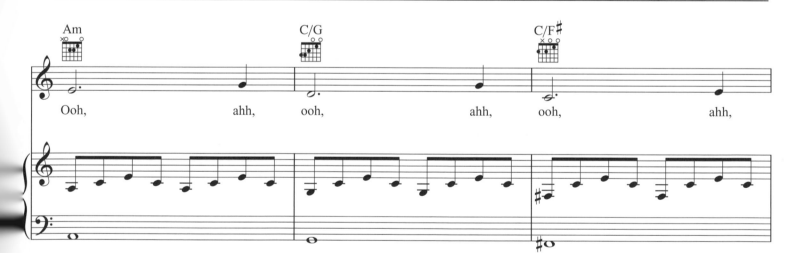

Ooh, ahh, ooh, ahh, ooh, ahh,

ooh. __ And won't __ this time. __

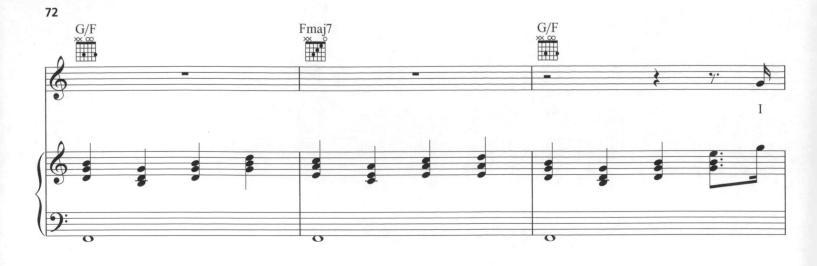

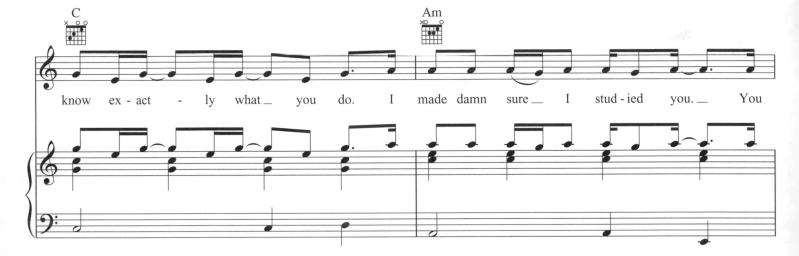

know ex-act-ly what __ you do. I made damn sure __ I stud-ied you. __ You

won't pick me, I am __ just a breeze un-der-neath your _____ wings. __ So

I pray each night __ you'll __ change your mind and may-be I _____ am worth __ the fight, __ but

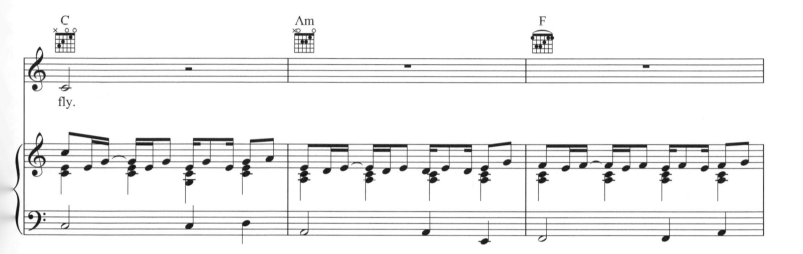

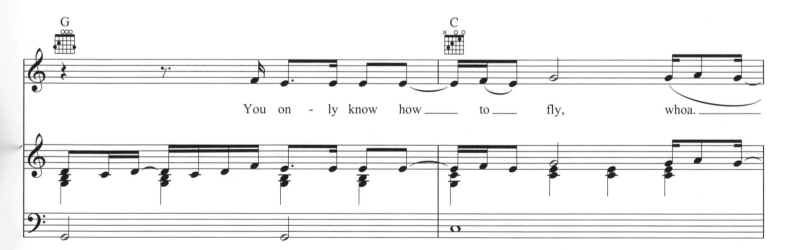

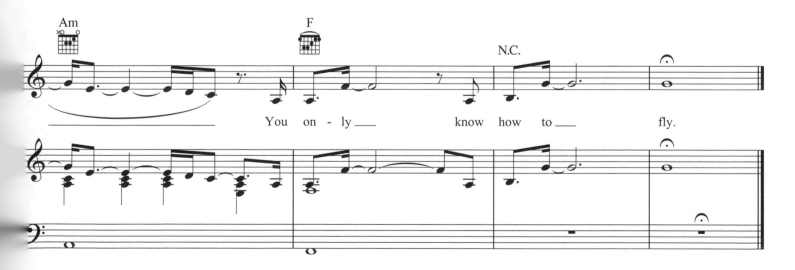

SHOT ME IN THE HEART

Words and Music by CHRISTINA PERRI
and JAMIE SCOTT

Copyright © 2013 Miss Perri Lane Publishing and EMI Music Publishing UK Ltd.
All Rights for Miss Perri Lane Publishing Administered by Songs Of Kobalt Music Publishing
All Rights for EMI Music Publishing UK Ltd. Administered by Sony/ATV Music Publishing LLC, 8 Music Square West, Nashville, TN 37203
All Rights Reserved   Used by Permission

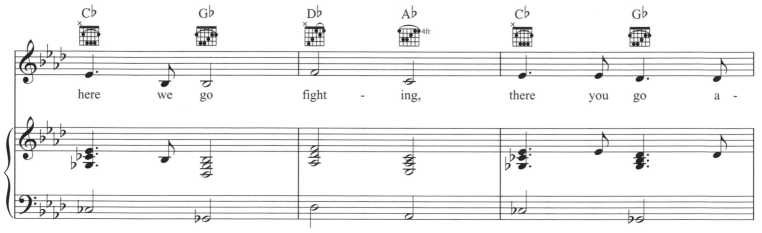

here we go fight - ing, there you go a -

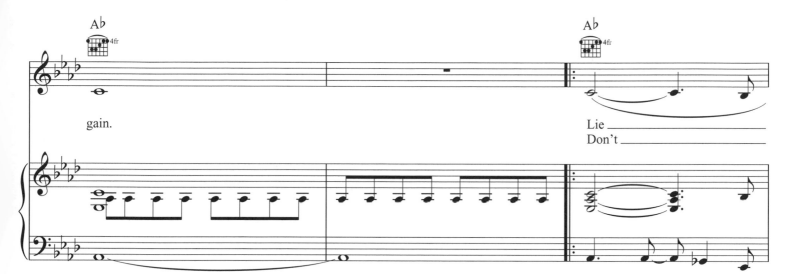

gain.

Lie _____

Don't _____

___ on _____ your own,   let this

___ call _____ me home,   you on - ly

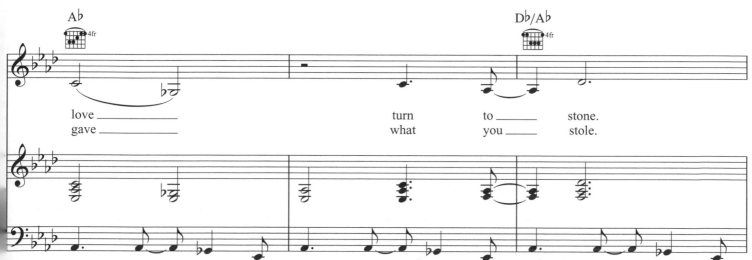

love _____   turn to _____ stone.

gave _____   what you _____ stole.

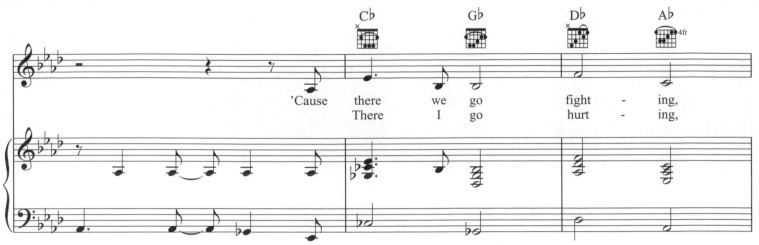

'Cause there we go fight - ing,
There I go hurt - ing,

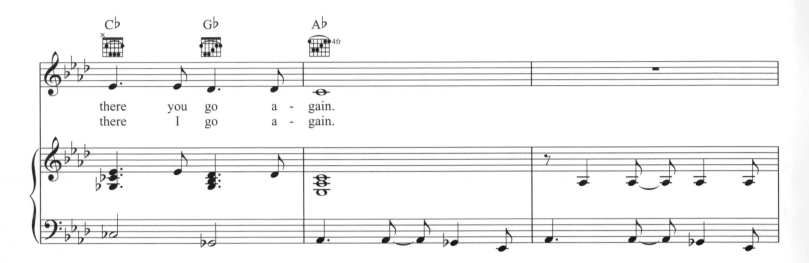

there you go a - gain.
there I go a - gain.

Here we go a - gain. }
Here we go a - gain. }

So

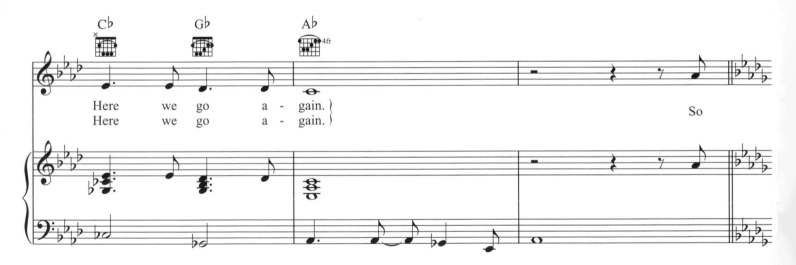

let me go, let___ me go, I don't know_ how we broke some-

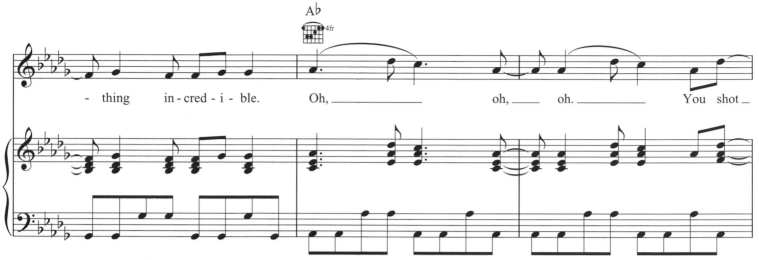

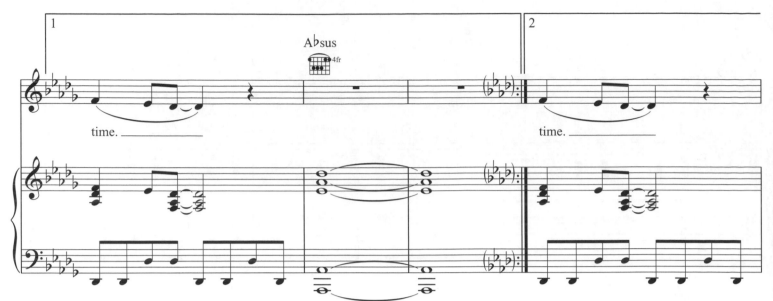

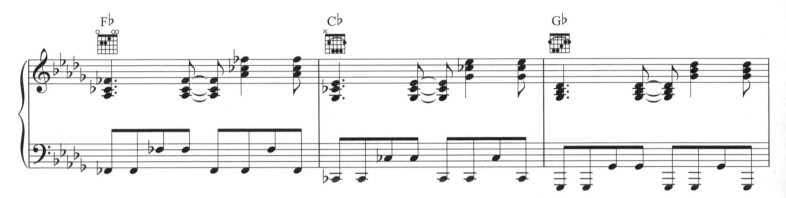

time. _____ I hope you know, hope _____ you know you let it go. _____

Lost it all, some - thing in - cred - i - ble. Oh, _____ oh, _

_____ oh. _____ You shot _____ me in the heart this time. _____ Shot _

_____ me in the heart this time. _____ Shot _____ me in the heart this time.

I BELIEVE

Words and Music by CHRISTINA PERRI
and DAVID HODGES

Copyright © 2014 Miss Perri Lane Publishing and 3 Weddings Music
All Rights Administered by Songs Of Kobalt Music Publishing
All Rights Reserved   Used by Permission

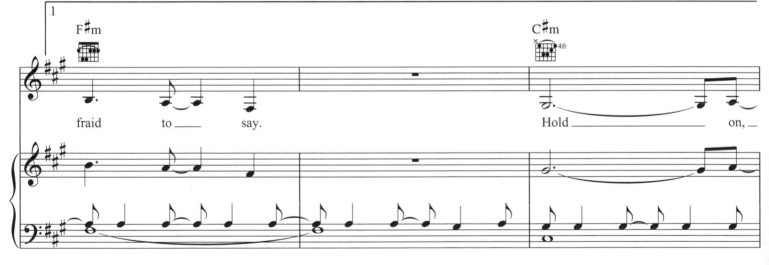

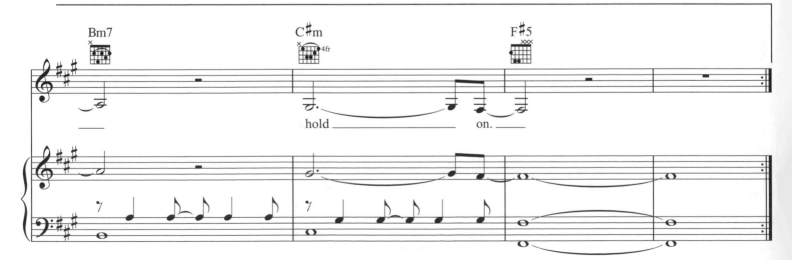

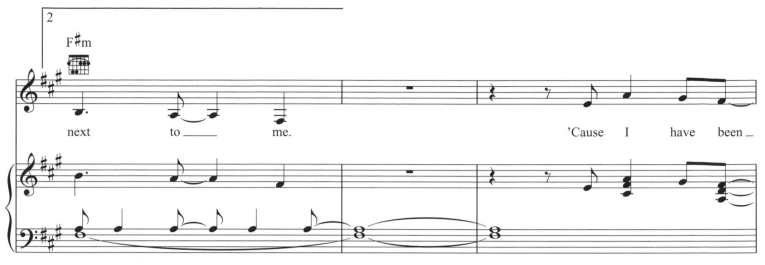

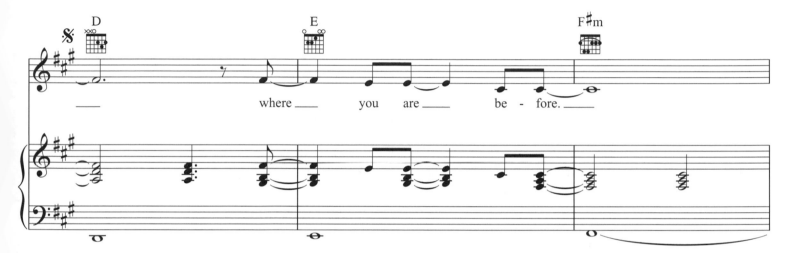

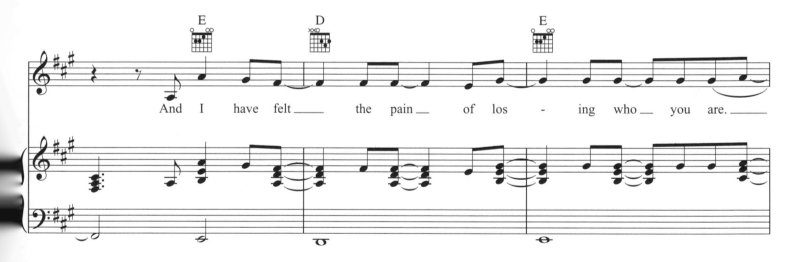

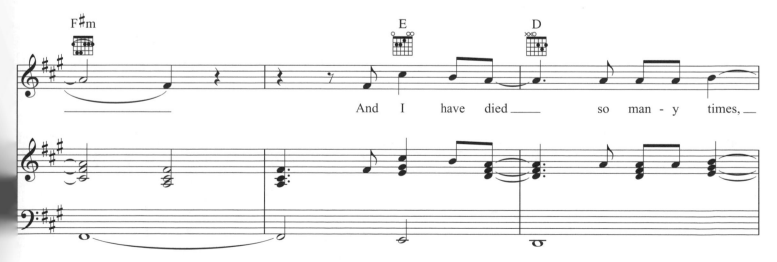

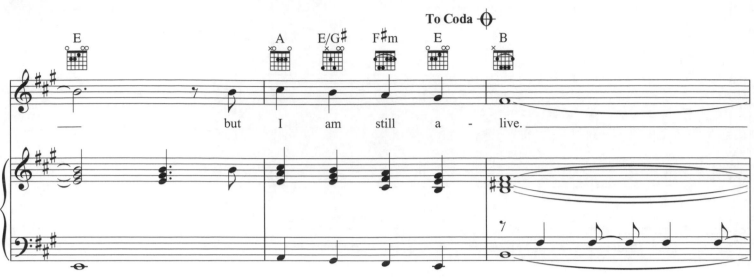

but I am still a - live.

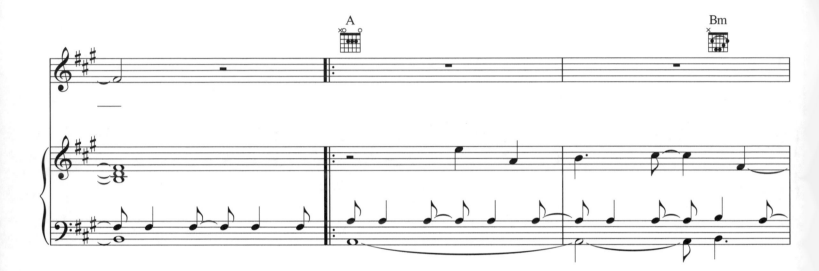

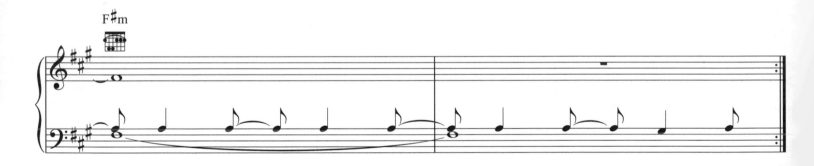

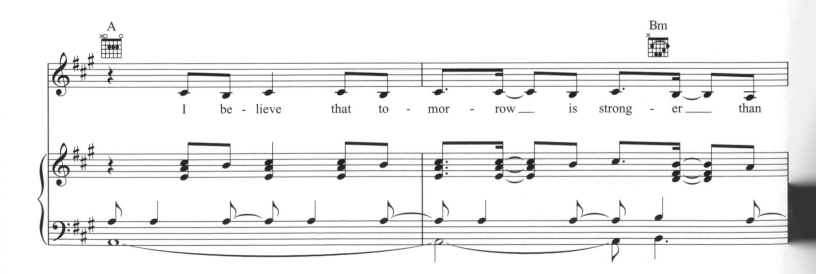

I be - lieve that to - mor - row ___ is strong - er ___ than

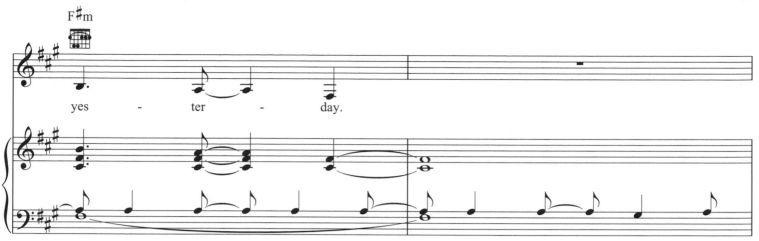

yes - ter - day.

And I be - lieve that your head is the on - ly thing

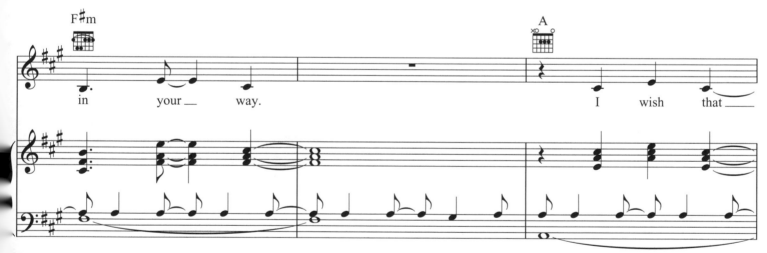

in your __ way. I wish that ___

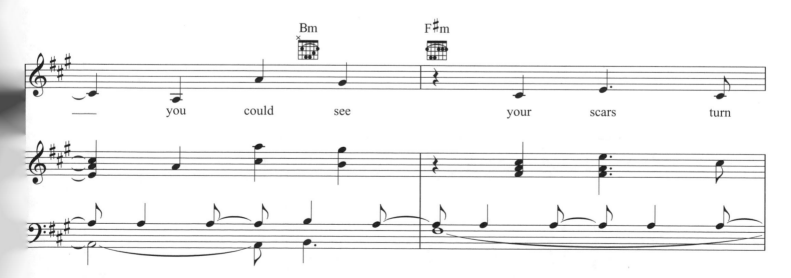

__ you could see your scars turn

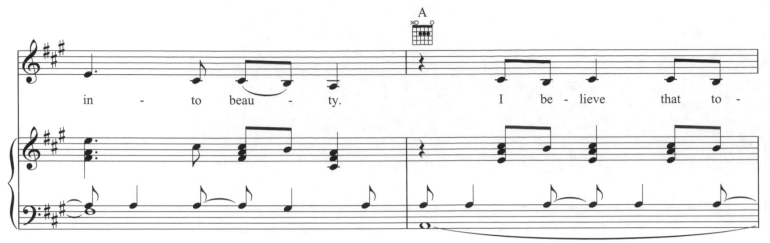

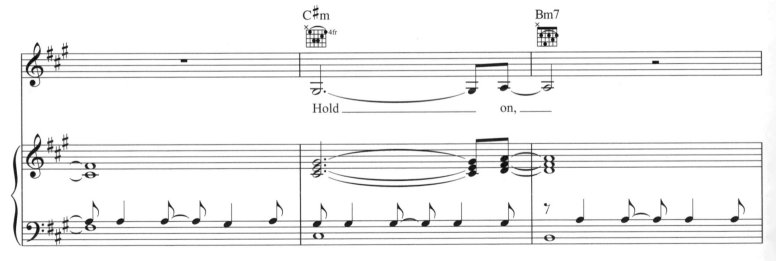

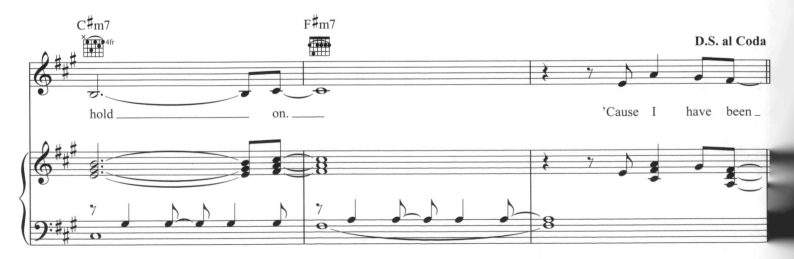

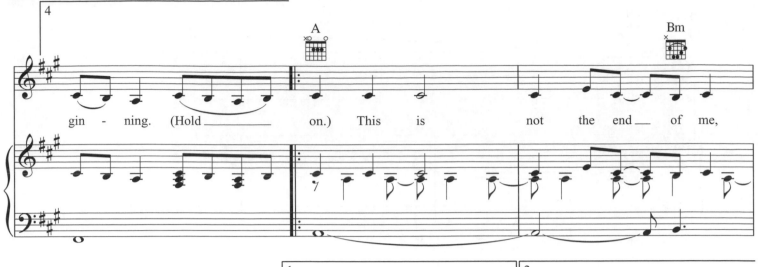

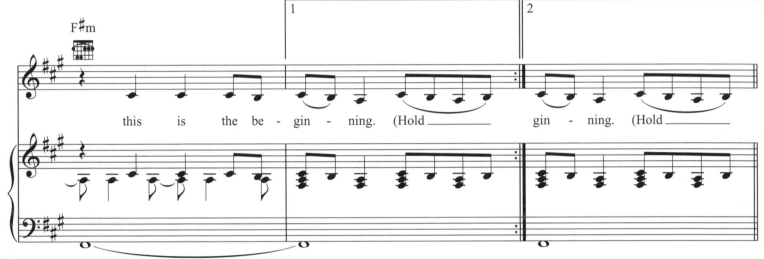